Steps on the Stone Path

Also by Robert Sardello

Facing the World with Soul

The Power of the Soul: Living the Twelve Virtues

Freeing the Soul from Fear

Love and the World: A Guide to Conscious Soul Practice

Love and the Soul: Creating a Future for Earth

Silence: The Mystery of Wholeness

Steps on the Stone Path

Working with Crystals and Minerals as a Spiritual Practice

Robert Sardello

Foreword by Robert Simmons

Goldenstone Press
Benson, North Carolina

North Atlantic Books
Berkeley, California

Published by Goldenstone Press and North Atlantic Books
P.O. Box 12327
Berkeley, California 94712

Cover art and cover design by Adam Chittenden
Book design by Brad Greene
Printed in the United States of America

Steps on the Stone Path: Working with Crystals and Minerals as a Spiritual Practice is sponsored by the Society for the Study of Native Arts and Sciences, a nonprofit educational corporation whose goals are to develop an educational and cross-cultural perspective linking various scientific, social, and artistic fields; to nurture a holistic view of arts, sciences, humanities, and healing; and to publish and distribute literature on the relationship of mind, body, and nature.

North Atlantic Books' publications are available through most bookstores. For further information, visit our Web site at www.northatlanticbooks.com or call 800-733-3000.

Library of Congress Cataloging-in-Publication Data

Sardello, Robert J., 1942–
    Steps on the stone path : working with crystals and minerals as a spiritual practice / Robert Sardello.
        p. cm.
    Includes bibliographical references.
    ISBN-13: 978-1-55643-898-1
    ISBN-10: 1-55643-898-2
    1. Crystals—Miscellanea. 2. Minerals—Miscellanea. 3. Spiritual life. I. Title.
    BF1442.C78S37 2010
    133'.2548—dc22
                                                                                            2009035219

3 4 5 6 7 8 9 10 VERSA 15 14 13 12 11 10

For Cheryl,
THE TRUE JEWEL OF THIS WORK

Acknowledgments

This book is unusual, even among the many unusual books on crystals. Richard Grossinger, thank you for immediately seeing that the writing may be of spiritual importance and encouraging me to complete what got off to a rocky start.

Hisae Matsuda, your care in seeing this book from manuscript to the form you now hold has been impeccable. You have a wonderful sense of a book as a Presence and not just a commodity.

Manjula Martin, thank you for your careful editing, your awareness of where I was reaching when I didn't even know it.

I am particularly grateful to you, Robert Simmons. You fanned the cooling embers of my years of interest in stones back into a true spiritual flame.

CONTENTS

FOREWORD

My eyes already touch the sunny hill
going far ahead of the road I have begun.
So we are grasped by what we cannot grasp;
it has its inner life, even from a distance—

and changes us, even if we do not reach it,
into something else, which, hardly sensing it,
     we already are;
a gesture waves us on, answering our own wave...
but what we feel is the wind in our faces.

—Rainer Maria Rilke, "A Walk"*

What you hold in your hands is the outline for a new spiritual path. When we think of a spiritual path, it is important to recognize that all true spiritual paths and practices change us, and they do so in ways that the person one believes oneself to be cannot predict or understand. When we begin, we cannot imagine the new, continually evolving being that the spiritual journey will lead us to become. This is different from the ideas implicit in most other books on the spiritual

---

*Robert Bly, James Hillman, and Michael Meade, *The Rag and Bone Shop of the Heart* (New York: Harper Perennial, 1993), 423.

qualities of stones, and in the sorts of work with stones that those books recommend. They tend to present a kind of recipe catalog, with the outcomes more or less assured. What Robert Sardello offers here is quite different. He invites the reader to shed his or her conditioning and enter unknown modes of perception, feeling, and spiritual activity, and to track this metamorphosis with a careful attention that is in itself a kind of transformation.

We are used to the familiar patterns of question and answer, desire and satisfaction. Those drawn to spiritual exploration with stones may for some length of time content themselves with these sorts of activities, where everything is more or less known beforehand. However, sooner or later we notice that something is missing, and we long for it without knowing what it is. In this book, you will find not an answer, but a beckoning, and if you follow it, you will learn that you have to exert yourself, just as you would in undertaking a journey in the outer world. In the course of the Stone Path, you will likely encounter difficulty and frustration, as well as wonder and love. Most certainly you will enter unknown territories, and you will encounter things utterly familiar—the stones—in ways that reveal how little about their spiritual nature was actually known.

In *Steps on the Stone Path*, one moves in a way that is rather like the person described in Rilke's poem above. In suggesting that we re-envision the stones as spiritual beings with whom we can relate, Sardello gives us a glimpse of where we are going. We see ahead into a new world where everything is spiritually alive—our "eyes already touch the sunny hill," though we have barely begun the journey. In following Sardello's line of thought, and in opening to the mysterious potential of meeting the stone beings *as they are*, rather than as our projections, we can feel a shift deep down, below the everyday ego and its habits. As in the poem, "we are grasped by what we cannot grasp." In reimagining the stones, we sense the vibrating inner life of the Earth herself, and we are changed. This change is indeed into what "we already are," since what is happening is an awakening to ourselves and the stones on the levels of soul and spirit. This is necessarily at the same time a constant activity of attentive awareness and participation in the unknown. Soul and spirit are larger than our everyday selves, and we cannot corral them into predictable parameters.

Here is where Sardello takes exception to most of the writings about the "spiritual properties of stones," which tend to quickly translate the inner experience of a stone's interaction with one's body and consciousness into familiar human concepts. Many authors have tended to take, for example, an incident of meditation in which the stone currents entered our hearts and kindled a delightful feeling, translating that into the promise that, "Rose Quartz can bring you love." Or we may feel something that gives rise to an image, which we change into a concept such as, "Cinnabar is a stone of abundance." Sardello has used many such statements to illustrate how the habits of egocentric conceptualization can cause us to whiz past the living mysteries of the Stone Beings. Our most common jump is the one we make to "what a stone can be used for." Implicit in this is the idea that "using" a stone is what we ought to do. Nowadays I make the analogy that it is also possible to view other people in terms of how we can "use" them, but we all know that in doing so we miss most of what a real relationship might offer—in both directions.

One of Robert Sardello's great gifts is this capacity to slow down the mental processes through careful inner observation. It was through discussions with him that I first realized that my own intuitive work in describing the stones' properties worked through images. As I meditated with various stones, I saw inner images, which I automatically translated into language so quickly that I went years without even noticing them.

The language was already a step away from the image, which was itself a step away from the immediate awareness of the vibrational "gestures" of the stones. Through the practices outlined in this book, we learn to track our journey into the worlds of the stones, into realms of amazing beauty, feeling, and holiness. To do this, we must bring ourselves into deep and reverential Silence, and into the sort of clear witnessing that is present to what presents itself, refraining from fantasy and projection. I have used versions of Sardello's practices in my most recent work, and they have greatly deepened my awareness of and my passion for what can happen through carefully and genuinely opening to the stones.

One of the radical ideas Sardello offers is that the appropriate attitude in our work with the stones is one of service and self-sacrifice. It is important to give up the idea of using the stones to gratify our desires, since their true purpose, and our opportunity for working with them, is of much greater significance. He tells us: "On this path, the desire to obtain these attributes [of the stones] for oneself has to be sacrificed, inwardly given away, again and again—for the sake of the angelic beings of the stones, for the sake of the spiritualizing of the Earth, and for the spiritualizing of the human being. Here, we are asked to admit that we do not know what is going on, that stones are spiritual teachers rather than servants of our desires—no matter how noble the desires might seem." Seeing this, we begin to understand why this work is envisioned as a spiritual path rather than a recipe book.

Such an insight might be accompanied by a certain pang of disappointment. We *like* to have our desires satisfied, and the friendly emanations of the stones and crystals we find in stores seem to promise such gratifications. They will even apparently perform such services for us, because, as spiritual beings, the stones are always offering themselves in love. I have befriended a piece of the stone Rosophia that soothes me to sleep whenever I need it, regardless of the stress levels of the day. Yet Sardello insists that we remain aware of the higher purpose to which we are called, with the stones and with the Earth: "The more recent part of the evolution of consciousness has been the very gradual development of the capacity to turn toward unification with the spiritual worlds.... Now is the time when we can freely participate in spiritualizing not only our own being, but also the being of the Earth." If, as he suggests, the Stone Path is uniquely suited for giving ourselves to this destiny, then continuing to view the stones as mere objects for our use is like using the Holy Grail for a beer mug.

Yet it is undeniable that we do benefit from taking the Stone Path journey. Just as in human relationship, the love we give rewards us with the experience of our own loving, whatever may be returned. And there is certainly a return when we enter into relationship with the Stone Beings—it's just that we can't know what it will be. Sardello offers a chapter on "Stones and the Circulation of Gifts" in which he states, "The primary purpose of the 'spiritual path of stones' is to develop a circulation between the earthly realms and the spiritual realms without assuming that we know what the angelic beings of the stones will bring to us." I stand with Sardello in asserting that we can and should trust this circulation without needing to know, in the same way we trust a friend or loved one, or in the way that our trust in the Divine is what we gesture, knowingly or not, with each breath and every heartbeat.

In the twenty-three years that I have been researching the nature of what goes on between human beings and the multitude of crystals and minerals to which we are attracted, I have noticed a few puzzles. One is the question of why people seem to universally sense that what goes on in the human/stone connection is necessarily *spiritual*. The delight that all of us who collect stones for their purported "energies" feel is a delight of *spiritual discovery*, whether we are conscious of it or not. The stones kindle within us the light and fire of spiritual potential, and this kindling is welcomed by our whole being.

Noticing this sheds some light on my second puzzle: If, as Sardello repeatedly points out, we think we are seeking out stones because we want to "get" for ourselves whatever properties that are ascribed to them, why are we not disappointed and disillusioned when the promised outcome of the recipe doesn't happen? I've seen this in myself and others for decades. We wear or meditate with one or many stones and we do not become rich, or suddenly enlightened, yet we still love the stones. Why? I believe Sardello touches on this when he suggests that we re-read the various stone encyclopedias, not as recipes with promised outcomes, but as metaphoric descriptions of the Stone Beings themselves. They don't *make us* rich or enlightened, but when we are with them, we are *in the presence* of those qualities, and much more.

The greatest gift of this book is that it works painstakingly to make us conscious of the true reasons for our attraction to the stones—the spiritual potential of both ourselves and the stones, and the possibilities of co-creative relationship with the stones and the Earth as spiritual beings. The refreshment we feel shows us that, like the walker in Rilke's poem, we are changing into what we already are.

When we enter the Silence and, following Sardello's clues along the path, encounter the worlds of the stones, we are met, astonishingly, by presences we felt but never knew. When we turn toward them in loving invitation, they indeed respond, and because they have real spiritual consciousness, we cannot know beforehand what the responses will be. Yet their gestures are unmistakable, and always serving what is for the good of the whole. As Rilke wrote, "a gesture waves us on, answering our own wave, but what we feel is the wind in our faces." That wind is the wave of awakening we experience as we realize that the stones, and the Earth, are alive.

That wind is joy.

Robert Simmons
January 12, 2010

INTRODUCTION

While meditative and healing work with crystals and minerals forms an essential, perhaps crucial, dimension of many spiritual practices, what *spiritually* happens when one is meditatively in the presence of the mineral world remains, for the most part, veiled. Accounts of the *process* whereby crystal workers come to the conclusions they do concerning the metaphysical and healing properties of stones are generally not available. Practitioners often describe "traveling" to other worlds through crystal meditations, but these accounts are usually directed toward gaining information concerning angelic beings, healing, past lives, or other experiences that may be useful for personal purposes. Nothing of the spirituality of crystals per se is of interest to most practitioners nor, for the most part, to those they serve. This approach is like discovering a new world and going there only to retrieve what seems valuable without bothering to look around and find out what the new land is like or how we might be of true service to that world.

If the mineral and crystal process of unfolding spiritual qualities can be carefully described, we can open up a new approach not only to the mineral world, but also to developing new contemplative practices that are particularly needed for the combined spiritual destiny of humanity and of the Earth.

This writing is based on a premise that the natural world is in communion with the cosmic world, and holds that a dynamic unity exists amongst Earth, Cosmos, and Humanity. Furthermore, this dynamic unity consists of the ongoing actions of spiritual presences ranging all the way from the Unknowable to the angels, the spirits, and the elemental beings. This book also holds that a particular importance in the functioning of this Whole is given to the spiritual and soul dimensions of the mineral world.

The mineral world is our ground, our basis, that upon which we live and rely. The narrowness of the present world-view relies not only on science, but on our being spectators of, rather than participants with, the Earth. Such a narrow view distracts us from considering the mineral world as a mode of consciousness rather than inert combinations of chemicals. Seeing the stones around us as simply inert chemical substances is an effect of a limited range of mental consciousness, the vibratory frequency of which allows us to perceive the world only as made up of dimensioned things separated from us and contrasting with our own inner lives.

This kind of consciousness does not provide the possibility of experiencing stones as forms and levels of consciousness. In order to open this possibility, it is necessary to attain a state of deep inner Silence matching the depth of the Silence of the stones themselves. It is not an impossible task.

Understanding how a crystal reveals its qualities inevitably takes us into larger questions. Where do crystals and minerals come from—not in terms of geology or mineralogy or chemistry, but spiritually? This question has to be answered, or at least approached, otherwise the field of working with stones is left open to the severe and just criticism that the "spiritual" properties of stones are no more than the psychic projections of those making claims concerning what stones can do for us. There is simply no way in which inert substances—which stones are considered to be by the physical sciences—are able to convey anything like active spiritual qualities to one who holds and inwardly listens to them. There must be more to stones than science can account for. Every worker with stones intuitively knows this is so.

Not enough attention has been given to the fact that when anything, including the practice of working with stones, is approached out of the sole realm of desire— that is, with the intention of getting something that one wants or needs—then the astrality, the lower levels of the spiritual domains, of that intent is bound to entangle personal conscious and subconscious desires with what actually happens. Projection abounds. Desire, which is inevitably oriented toward the "me," prevents the union of our spiritual being with the spiritual being of the stones. Particular and somewhat difficult spiritual preparation and practices are needed in order to go beyond the astral or unexamined soul dimensions in working with stones. A shift from "willfulness to get" to "willingness to receive" is necessary in working with the subtle realms of stone consciousness. With this shift we can access the freedom that comes about by consciously releasing the grasping will and entering the domain of willingness to be with the grace of the spiritual worlds.

This viewpoint is no different than one would find in any seriously established form of esoteric and spiritual practice. What is new is the application of these basic spiritual principles to the domain of the stone worlds—and the spiritual and earthly significance of doing so.

CHAPTER I
Entering Stone-Awareness

The plethora of metaphysical books on stones share one common characteristic: a compendium of crystals and minerals is given, encyclopedic in character, that lists the stones and what they are supposed to do, which is inevitably to enhance some quality that one would like to have, heal an illness one is experiencing, open a center of spiritual consciousness, or change oneself in some imagined favorable way. Work with crystals is somewhat more advanced in that certain "spiritual" technologies have been developed for meditating with different kinds of crystals in order to produce different effects.

The understanding of what actually happens in the presence of crystals and minerals is confined to explanations usually employing the rather abstract term "energy." Sometimes scientific explanations or speculations in scientific terms are attempted; such "explanations" are typically speculative, borrowing from scientific work in other fields that is then applied to stones. That is, there is no "science," not even an inner science, of the metaphysical working with stones based on the stones themselves. Sometimes spiritual explanations are given—that is, the felt effect is attributed to angels or spirit guides, or related to a certain star or galaxy. These spiritual explanations have a fiat character—the reader of such material is called upon to believe what is said in spite of the fact that, most often, no context is given for indicating that particular angelic beings or spirit guides are connected with certain stones.

These cautions are not intended to be negative criticisms. In fact, these ways of working with stones imply that each individual is invited to become his or her own researcher; each person must dive in and find out for themselves.

In addition, there is an inherent self-interest in "spiritually" working with the mineral world insofar as the interest is in what crystals and minerals can do for us. While interest in "spiritual" work with stones comes almost exclusively out of the New Age movement, the approach is decidedly from the past. For there is complete reliance, a kind of faith, that a crystal or a stone will bring something one needs—much in the same fashion as prayers or religious rituals that have become more and more egotistically oriented toward providing what an individual wants and needs. A *truly* "new age" approach to crystals would approach the human being as a spiritual being acting in cooperation with spiritual stone-consciousness of crystals, rather than hiding old-time religion under a new rubric. Our present and future ages concern developing the capacities of acting and living like spiritual human beings rather than like human beings who now and then do spiritual things, such as listen to crystals, while the rest of our lives remain caught in the deadliness of rank materialism.

Robert Simmons is one of the few thinkers and practitioners working with stones who has become interested in a larger framing of the question of why stones are helpful and how it is possible to experience their effects. The most interesting and unusual aspect of Simmons's work is that he is a true explorer of subtle domains through crystals and minerals. And he intuits very clearly that crystals and minerals have a central role to play in the spiritual evolution of humanity and the spiritualization of the Earth. In my opinion, Simmons has explored the lore and esoteric dimensions of stones more than anyone. He has worked extensively with the Grail legend in relation to stones and with the centrality of the spiritual presence known as Sophia, the Soul of the World, who is said to be guardian of the earth realm. He has also worked to understand and develop practices with stones that provide access to the human Body of Light. His willingness—indeed, his sense of urgency—in working with stones and seeking to understand them as spiritual beings has inspired me to engage in this search alongside him.[1]

I have been interested in minerals and crystals since childhood, and have collected them for more than fifty years. The gateway to entering into a more spiritual approach to stones than is currently available comes from the still-felt sense of wonder that we experienced as children in relation to the mineral world. I still vividly remember feeling wholly at one with the natural world, particularly with hills and mountains, and the stones. And I remember holding my first special stone, which I found in a small cave in Colorado. There was an enlivening of *sensing* that occurred; the stone glowed in my hand; it was a living being; it was as if a traveler from afar were offering itself in intimate friendship. And I lived an inner connection with this stone for a long time. I still have it, and it still retains its mysterious presence as a living being. One can work spiritually with a single stone for a very long time; it can become one's spiritual teacher. The compendium approach tends to stimulate egotistical "wants" and holds out promises of getting what we desire. The notion of a single stone, or a few stones, as spiritual teachers goes in a different direction. The compendium may help one choose what kind of stones to work with, but once chosen, we can develop a long and intimate relationship with the being that is that stone. Such an attitude takes an inherent interest in the stone worlds we might innocently have, an interest that is waiting to be developed as a relationship with a spiritual companion. This approach retrieves that interest from the distraction of accumulating stones as commodities for our use.

When we were children, we had not yet developed the abstract intellectuality through which we separate ourselves from the outer world, nor had we experienced its result of veiling the immediate presence of the things of the world with concepts. Now, as adults, we can only perceive that which we have concepts to perceive. I may say, for example, that I am looking at a tree; however, "tree" is already a concept, and veils the particularity of what is being sensed. Even more, our concepts are impoverished and severely limited to materialistic concepts. If, for example, a compendium of stones says that a particular stone stimulates the third eye, that way of speaking predetermines what we are able to experience, as all concepts do. If, on the other hand, based on a compendium of stones, I choose to work with a stone that initiates an *inner feeling*, the compendium has served as an introduction to a spiritual being rather than a predetermined conclusion concerning what should happen.

We are unable to perceive a stone as a spiritual presence in large measure because we conceive of a stone as an inert object, a dead, material thing. We are thus deeply moved and excited, and puzzled, when we pick up a stone and actually feel something from it. We allow this slight invitation to find a way out of a materialistic conceptualization of matter to be the indicator that something of a more subtle nature is going on; that, somehow, this "dead matter" has magical properties. The immediate, sensory investigation of what might be happening, though, tends to be covered over by theories of chakras being stimulated, auras activated, energy transferred. None of these notions derive from giving loving attention to the stone itself, who gives itself freely and completely, allowing itself to be "imagined" in any way we want to do so, waiting silently to be seen for Who it is.

First, we have to work on our concepts and bring them into coherence with what we actually experience and sense. We have to work on our sensing, to be conscious in our sensing so that we are not led around by preformed concepts. And we have to find a way to speak and write so that the coherence between what we think and what we perceive become one. Then the true living, spiritual beings of the minerals will begin to reveal themselves.

A word also needs to be said about spirituality. The spiritual approach to crystals and minerals taken here is one that is contemplative, embodied, in connection with the Earth; works through the medium of soul life and the interior of the heart; and does not seek to be removed from earthly existence in favor of "enlightenment" or being absorbed into the "All." The tradition from which such a spirituality finds roots is the esoteric Grail tradition, and, in a more contemporary way, is indebted to the work of Rudolf Steiner. It also stems from the work of C. G. Jung and, most of all, from phenomenology, which is the art of letting the appearance of something in the world—or some interior presence, feeling, or quality—reveal itself on its own terms rather than imposing theories or our preconceived notions on it.

When we hold a stone in our hand, one that we felt drew our attention, it is worthwhile considering not "what" drew our attention here, but "Who" drew our attention. The stone itself is like an icon of nature. An icon is something very different than a spiritual and artistic picture to look at. An icon looks at us. In the presence of an icon, we feel "seen"; it is as if someone, the figure of the icon in its spiritual being, perceives us as we perceive that figure. This is also the way it is with a precious stone. The word "precious" here does not mean "of monetary value." It instead describes our immediate sensory experience of the stone, our felt sense that when we hold the stone, the stone addresses us in its own "language"—a wordless language we must then learn to be with on its own terms rather than seek to translate what it is revealing into already-familiar concepts.

Entering into a working relationship with stones by means of careful seeing—freed from unconscious assumptions, preformed concepts, and, most of all, our individual desires—is an instance of what Rudolf Steiner calls the "new Yoga of Light."[2] Yoga means "divine connection." In previous times, Steiner says, the spirit existed primarily within the element of air. Thus, the prevalence of the yoga of breathing in India, for it was through the control of the breath that one came into connection with the Divine. Now, however, the spirit exists in an intense way in the element of light. Here is what Steiner says of this shift:

To the extent that we conceive of light as being the general representative of sense-perception, we must bring ourselves to think of light as ensouled—just as it was self-evident for people of the second and third pre-Christian millennia to think of the air as ensouled (as indeed it was). We must thoroughly overcome the habit of viewing light in the ways that our material-istic age is accustomed to do. We must completely ban-ish the notion that only those vibrations of which modern physics and the general consciousness of humanity speak today emanate from the sun. We must become clear that soul pours through cosmic space on pinions of light.[3]

We are given here the seeds of a method of approach-ing stones in such a manner that their consciousness, their soul/spirit beings will reveal themselves to us in a direct way that allows us to inwardly know we are in direct spiritual connection with the stones. If we are unable to perceive stones spiritually, to be with them in a fully sensory way that is also spirit-sensing, then surely they cannot reveal themselves spiritually. So we are condemned to mere speculations, trying to make a case for the spiritual being of stones without the right and needed equipment.

To reiterate, there is a difference between utilizing stones to gain spiritual qualities and abilities, and heal-ing and working with stones *as a spiritual path.* This book attempts to introduce the latter. It is as if all previous work with stones has been a preparation for this moment of the evolution of consciousness. Stones are difficult to find the way into. In the ancient mystery schools, the highest and most difficult work was that of entering into the world of stones. Like in alchemy, with stones there is a "Lesser Work" and a "Greater Work." There is no evaluation entailed in these terms; they are descriptive terms. Before one can go on to be with the matter of the world in a spiritual way, it is necessary to engage in a transformative preparation by simply being with matter in a completely open and receptive way. Almost all previous writing remains with stones in an outer, though receptive way; the interior life of the stone is felt, but not entered into. The effect of the stone is felt, but not its interior being. This is the "Lesser Work," and it is completely necessary. This writing introduces one way to approach "The Greater Work." The Greater Work consists of entering into the interior of matter, making connection with its soul and spirit, and developing the capacities needed for inwardly perceiving indications of its soul and spirit— and becoming physically altered by this way of being with living substance.

A stone is a definite form of substance-consciousness. It is not "dead matter." It is a living being. But we have to learn to connect with it through its mode of consciousness, and not expect to understand it through our usual kind of consciousness, or through a mode of connection that is wholly oriented toward getting something from the contact. We can learn to experience something entirely unknown from a crystal or mineral when we refrain from immediately translating that mystery into our known concepts. For example, by simply saying that a stone—say, Rose Quartz—stimulates love, we are taking what the stone is doing and translating it into concepts that we are completely familiar with. Our pre-given concept has covered what is trying to reveal itself. In this now accepted way of working with stones, our consciousness is not structurally altered at all, and the stone consciousness has been constrained to speak our language of concepts. If the Rose Quartz does resonate love, it is the resonance of an entirely unknown and unfamiliar mode of love, a new soul dimension, one capable of transforming our very being if we remain open to such a possibility.

That stones are forms of autonomous consciousness that are unfamiliar to us, that do not reveal themselves as familiar to our consciousness, is not a theory. I will try to describe as clearly as I can something of the way stone-consciousness works. To do so requires that we empathetically enter into their form of consciousness as much as we can. Otherwise, there is no bridge to connect our being with that of the stone. Such an approach has a long, long history. The seventeenth-century Japanese poet Matsuo Bashō gave this advice to his students:

Go to the pine if you want to learn about the pine, or to the bamboo if you want to learn about the bamboo. And in doing so, you must let go of your subjective preoccupation with yourself. Otherwise you impose yourself on the object and don't learn. Your poetry arises by itself when you and the object have become one, when you have plunged deep enough into the object to see something like a hidden light glimmering there.[4]

To enter into the interior life of stones requires that we do so by entering our own interiority, and from there, forming a unity with the interiority of the stones. Then, the stone-consciousness will begin to reveal itself—but not in terms of concepts and words that come from our personality, which are totally foreign to such a deep and mysterious presence. We listen to such worlds by being formed by them more than being in-formed by them. We learn by being transfigured through and through, in body, mind, and soul—and in ways that are impossible to know in advance. As with starting any spiritual path, if one is not willing to lose a sense of control, it is far better to have never started at all.

The precious stones themselves give us a first clue of what we must do; we must enter into the deepest possible Silence.[5] (To distinguish this Holy Silence from ordinary silence, in what follows I will capitalize Silence as a way of indicating that it is the presence of a being or beings and not simply the absence of sound.) That is what strikes us most clearly about a stone—its Silence. When we hold a stone and attend to it even slightly, the nature of this Silence begins to reveal something of itself. It is something much, much deeper than what we would usually interpret as the absence of a capacity to communicate. This Silence is very alive and very active. The Silence of a stone does not mean only that it is without noise or sound. Silence is not the absence of sound; it is a palpable quality. When, for example, we take a walk in a beautiful forest, we are suddenly surrounded by the presence of living Silence, and feel intimately in connection with a Holy presence. When we attentively hold a stone, beings of Silence stand with us at the threshold where we enter into the deeper reality of the mineral world. This entrance cannot be bypassed; it is the gateway between worlds, and as such is also the connector of worlds, through which it becomes possible to enter into unity with the stone-beings.

It seems, perhaps, a huge step from experiencing the Holy Silence of a stone to speaking of "stone-beings"; we have yet to notice other qualities of particular stones to actually begin to feel the presence of "beings." I've jumped slightly ahead here in the attempt to convey something of the nature of the Silence encountered with a stone and to draw attention to the soul's experience of the Silence rather than a rational intellectual notion of silence as the absence of sound. Given the Silence of stone, we can develop stone-awareness by developing the capacity of silencing the mind. The simplest and most direct way is given in a meditation by Satprem, friend and colleague of influential yogis Sri Aurobindo and the Mother.[6] The practice concerns silencing the usual thought-organization that constantly plagues us. Try for a few moments to stop thinking—completely. It is likely that you find this task quite impossible. The attempt, though, is instructive. Notice, for example, how thinking is identified with the body: when we try to stop thinking we feel an inward anxiety and then a panic. Notice also how thinking inserts itself from seemingly out of nowhere. We find ourselves well along the way of thinking before we even recognize we are thinking.

When we concentrate on a stone, the concentration seems to take care of the intrusion of thinking. It does not. The concentration is continually being interrupted by thoughts about the stone that may seem to be what the stone is saying. It may indeed be that the stone is revealing itself, but what it reveals is constantly being organized by our familiar ways of thinking. The first contribution made by Satprem in his interpretation of Sri Aurobindo is to show that usual thinking is a narrow band of vibration, a frequency that makes possible our experiencing the world as we do. Usual thinking is an organizing frequency that puts what reveals itself into subject-object consciousness. If the frequency, the vibration, is extended and expanded, then we begin to experience things we usually cannot experience; and we find that we cannot translate what we experience back into the categories of usual thinking without severely limiting what is experienced. To begin working to expand vibrational consciousness, Satprem suggests this practice: we cannot simply stop thinking. We have to give usual consciousness something to occupy its attention.

Imagine that you are floating on a clear, calm, lake. Enter into this imagination so vividly that indeed you begin bodily to feel that you are floating on a clear, calm lake. When you find yourself leaving this imagination, return to it. Then, there is a second part to the practice. This practice is to be taken into daily life;

it is not something for moments of meditation only. Wherever you are, whatever you are doing, try to enter into this imagining. It does not interfere with what you are doing; in fact, it will enhance it considerably, because new ways will come to you, ways beyond your usual thinking.

This practice is an invaluable preparation for spiritual work with stones. Indeed, the practice has to become so inwardly integrated that it is an essential part of our lives. As we become more accustomed to what it is like to be a more open vibration of consciousness, we become more open to the vibratory qualities of stones. More importantly, we become more able to refrain from letting our usual forms of thinking intrude while we are working spiritually with stones. These intrusions seem to be revelations from the stones; they are not. Rather, the intrusions are ordinary thinking-consciousness forms of organization that allow us to say something about the stones, relieving the anxieties that stem from losing control of thinking as we know it.

Different crystals and minerals are accompanied by different qualities of Silence. The introverted Silence of a dark blue-gray Chalcedony differs from the self-contained and yet openly shared Silence of a beautiful Aquamarine. The exuberant, bright, sparkling

Silence of Azeztulite differs from the calm, deep Silence of Rosophia. The Silence of a perfectly water-clear Quartz crystal is even different, for example, from the Silence of a Quartz crystal that is somewhat clouded. The Silence of the water-clear crystal has qualities of utter stillness, perfect receptivity; it is a Silence unknown in this earthly world, like a visitation of cosmic Silence. The cloudy Quartz crystal has the Silence of tension within it; the kind of Silence that comes with color—is dynamic in movement and somewhat easier to connect with—deep, to be sure, but not a "transparent" Silence that we can be within and allow to permeate every fiber of our being with spiritual clarity. There is more "earth" to the Silence of the clouded and the colored crystals. They have their own mysteries, so this is not an evaluation of one as being better than the other. In befriending a stone, the attempt is to help us be fully present with the unique character of Who the stone is.

These qualities show through the sensory presence of the stones, but are beyond usual sensory qualities. Once we feel these differing qualities of Silence, we find the unified soul connection with the stones. We find that the stones then actually change. They begin to "speak" to us, as if they were sleeping or hiding until they were addressed in terms appropriate to them.

This step of entering into the Silence with stones cannot be bypassed without guaranteeing that what we discover has more to do with our own unconscious wishes and desires than it does with what the stones offer. Silence is both the stones' mode of presence and also the language of reverence with which they are to be addressed. One can spend a lot of time with stones just being with their Silence, looking for nothing more. More, of course, is offered in the Silence and can be felt, wordlessly, as an invitation into our interior with the interior of the stones. "Interior" here does not mean "inside" or "hidden from view." The interior is something completely visible, providing we have opened ourselves sufficiently. Finding interiority through Silence shifts us from being spectators of stones into having a felt connection with them. There is often an emotional response when this connection occurs. We may feel waves of closeness, a deep aesthetic response, an inward gulp of joy, or even tears. It is important to let the emotion pass, as that is not the stone's connection with us as much as it is our isolated soul's surprise at finding an interior connection with something that the mind usually considers, at best, a collectible item.

Our first gesture toward a stone is thus to enter into its Silence. It is a way of getting acquainted with stones, like a first intimate meeting. Just as we get to know the soul of a person when we sit with them in intimate Silence, we get a felt-sense of the soul of a stone through being with it in loving Silence and reverence. There is a difference, though, between getting to know stones and getting to know people. The soul of the stone relies much more on our initial gesture of meeting it half-way, with our soul-presence, than does a person. It is a little like trying to approach someone who has been abused. It takes a great deal of inner presence, patience, and love toward that person. A stone can be mistaken for dead matter because most often we neglect the gesture of meeting the stone as soul-being. In its incredible depth of Silence, in what seems to us to be a deep, endless sleeping state, the stone partakes of the Silence of the Universe itself. Notice that if we look at a picture of one of the great galaxies, we are filled not only with awe by the beauty of the galaxy; we are also filled with the same qualities of Silence as when we carefully and lovingly give our attention over to a stone.

When we carefully perceive a stone, we experience the deeds of the spiritual worlds. We perceive those deeds from within the earth element, but feel the activity of the gods. That is, what exists in the Cosmos as the currents, forces, and wordless beauty of the gods—what

the Christian tradition calls the creating "angels"—
we perceive in the precious stones. Rudolf Steiner puts
it this way:

---

*Here we have a quartz crystal, a six-sided prism
enclosed by six-sided pyramids; here we have a salt
crystal that might be cube-shaped, here a pyrite crystal that might be dodecahedron. We look at all of this
. . . and can only say to ourselves: Out there in the
universe exists essential being. For us the salt crystal
is the manifestation of something that permeates in
an essential way all of space, a world in itself. We
look at the pyrite crystal, likewise cubic or dodecahe-
dral. We say to ourselves: in the cosmos something
exists that fills all of space; for us the crystal is an
expression or the manifestation of an entire world.
We look at many entities, each of which encloses a
world in itself. And here we stand on earth and say to
ourselves: in the earth element we encounter the deeds
of many worlds. And when we human beings on earth
think and act, the thinking and doing of manifold
beings flows together into our thinking and doing. We
see in the immeasurably diverse crystal forms the rev-
elation of a great abundance of beings living out their
existence in spatial and mathematical figures. In the
crystals we are looking at the gods.*[7]

Here is a statement from one of the world's great clair-voyants and the developer of Spiritual Science indi-cating that with precious stones we have the presence of the gods (the angels, he also says elsewhere). We cannot expect, though, that the gods/angels will speak human language. The heavens don't know English, or German, or any other human language. It is up to us to enter into their mode of being and consciousness. This fact considerably complicates working with stones, but we can find at least an indirect way of understand-ing what the gods/angels are doing.

Precious stones, while being a gesture of the angels and their presence in an earthly way, are at the same time caught in the world of gravity and the world of coldness. A stone is simultaneously in both of these worlds—the presence of the spiritual world of the creating angels and the cold of the earth, of gravity, of the weight of the earth, which makes the stone appear enclosed in itself. Earth, of course, is also a living being, and is "cold" in its aspect of gravity; Earth no longer shines, but there is the potential for Her to do so again. That potential lies in the spiritual life of stones. The stones need us to perceive their warmth and creative gestures; they need us to per-ceive them in their spiritual being in order for them to be the fullness of themselves. We are the bridge that makes it possible for the earth-bound stone to fulfill its wholeness of a cosmic-earthly being. It is here where work with stones often falls short and risks getting caught in the limitations of egotism. Because we have the power, with the uncontrollable presence of grace, to return the stone to its wholeness by our loving attention, the moment we do turn our attention to a stone we feel the vast cosmic reality of the stone. But we but do not know what it is we are experiencing; we think the stone is giving us what we want or need.

To give our attention to stones without expecting a direct response, a direct giving of what we need, requires entering the *spiritual path of stone work*. If we experience a first meeting with a stone and then take for ourselves what is offered, we have closed the door to that path. For some, that is fine; they are not called to this spiritual path, and their attention to a crystal or mineral makes no significant difference in their life. Others, though, are drawn to more, but cannot find what this "more" consists of because it has not been addressed. This attraction, felt inwardly as "there is more that I am to be doing with stones," is an inner invitation to take up this initiatory path where what one receives from the worlds of stones is much more mysterious and completely tied in with what one gives to the spiritual worlds and also to what we are spiritually able to give to the future of the Earth.

Stones indeed do serve us. Seen from within the Stone Path, there is more to them than giving us certain gifts. The gifts of stones, as now described by the many compendia of stones, are but an invitation to work with them in their Wholeness as part of a heaven-earth-human unity. When we find our way into that Wholeness, new gifts are offered. These new gifts are not given in a way that addresses our wants, desires, and needs while bypassing the most significant and vital work to be done with stones. Instead, they are invitations to return stones to their angelic Wholeness. When that part of the spiritual work occurs, there is circulation back to the earthly world. There will be a return, an answer from the gods, from the angels. But it will be a spiritual answer, an unexpected answer, not a predictable one like those offered by the compendia of stones like a department store display of spiritual goodies.

CHAPTER 2

The Sensory Yoga of Stones

The term "yoga" refers to union with the self and the divine self. There are many ways to seek such a connection. I do not believe I am misusing the word "yoga" by suggesting that meditative work with stones can indeed be one of the paths to the Divine. Further, I want to convey from the outset that the Stone Path is not easy and requires dedication. In order to get to know stones, which when recognized in their cosmic and earthly wholeness will respond to us, we have to develop the capacity of entering into an inner state in which we are able to listen and truly hear the stones' way of responding. The very first, practical aspect of this approach to stones is the work of becoming accustomed to and aware of the gestures of the crystals and stones. It is something that happens very immediately when, for example, we are in a shop looking at stones or out in the natural world paying attention to them. There is something about the stone that is weightless, and there is a kind of translucency to the stone—even if it is opaque. In the Silence, it is as if we are invited to see into a stone. We can feel the stone. When given loving attention, the stone lifts us out of the heaviness of a materialistic existence and we feel something of its spiritual world. It is perhaps not so much that we are attracted to a stone, as is often said to be the case, but rather that the spiritual force of the stone can be noticed when our attention is not focused in its usual intellectual way.

When met in the overlapping region of Silence, stones carefully begin to reveal themselves. Small aspects of a stone begin to stand out. I have an Azeztulite stone that has the tiniest of tiny bright spots of light toward the center. Every time I look at the stone, this light shines intensely, as if there were a sun deep inside the stone. Crystal faces begin to be noticed—not simply as interesting forms, but as gestures. Rudolf Steiner says:

And it belongs to the most beautiful things that can be experienced by a person who wants to practice the particulars of occult reading, that this person experiences the mineral world in such a way that everywhere he gradually assimilates the infinitely diverse gestures of the spiritual entities of nature in the shape of its separating surfaces, its delineating edges, and its characteristic relations to the external cosmos; in translucency, transparency, and in the crystalline brightness of rock crystal, quartz, calcite, emerald, and chrysoprase....[8]

Majestic mountains of silvery-red metallic Cinnebar, almost-achieved fluidity, arise from snowy white plates of Calcite, constituting the small stone resting on my desk. I wonder what this mineral form is doing here, coming together in this way? A small piece of Rhodochrosite, deep red and transparent, in multiple plates, embraces a small, shiny bit of a metal, perhaps lead, on one edge. The juxtaposition of these two minerals brings images of another world. When viewed through the resonating Silence, any stone already hints at the presence of other worlds, unmistakably spiritual worlds, held here by the gravity of earth but still filled with cosmic resonance. The more we are present with stones in the Great Silence, the more each stone reveals, through the way our souls reach out into the Silence, something of its spiritual mystery.

The feeling that we are in the presence of something special will not last. If we simply buy the stone or pick it up from the Earth, take it home, and put it on the shelf, for the most part it returns to its unattended coldness. It can and does come alive again when we give it loving, perceptual attention. If we start trying to squeeze the quality out of it that the various compendia of stones say it has, we get something from the stone for a while and then move on to the next new stone and its advertised qualities. We may have gotten something from the stone, but it received nothing from us. In essence, we contribute to its death.

Let's look for a moment more closely at a Quartz crystal as an example. Here we try to see that we are meeting the presence of angelic beings who have come into the Earth, long ago, and contributed not only to the forming of the Earth, but to creative angelic beings who also contributed to the spiritual and physical evolutions of the human being. This latter, *the forming of the human being,* is crucial. If we, in some manner, did not have within us something of the spiritual essence of the Whole of the mineral world, then we could not come into union with the world of crystals and minerals. We would not have the potential within us to do so. This principle of sensing the things of the world is well known in the esoteric tradition. Seeing, for example, is not just a matter of receiving light from what we look at. A more subtle, etheric light goes out from our eye to meet the light that issues from the object. We cannot sense the interior quality of a crystal or mineral except through the gift that the mineral worlds have contributed to us: our engagement in the coevolution of the Earth and the human being.

We have a view of evolution that assumes the Earth evolved first, then the plants, then the animals, and then, finally, human beings arrived, or perhaps evolved from the monkey. One of Rudolf Steiner's greatest contributions was his clairvoyant recognition that Earth and human beings evolved and are still evolving—together, as one process. If this view, which is not a theory but a seeing, is meditated upon, we quickly come to see that working contemplatively with the mineral world assumes, though we have not yet known it, this intimate relation between the Earth and the human being—and indeed, the whole of the Cosmos.

When we look at the six sides and the pyramid top of a clear Quartz crystal, we are looking at the convergence of spiritual currents from the Cosmos. We think that crystals grow from the ground up, but that is not quite true. The substances for a crystal occur within the ground—even there, it is important to try and imagine these substances as spiritual forces rather than chemicals—but the form of the crystal itself comes from the merging of currents of force out of the vast Cosmos flowing together and meeting. If we go to the mountains and find a crystal, we will find that it sits on its bottom. This spatial orientation, however, is due to gravity and is not an indication that the crystal grew from the earth outward: crystal *form* develops from the Cosmos inward. The mathematical exactness of crystal form is the clue here that a cosmic process is involved. Sacred geometry recognizes the

five Platonic solids as the formative shaping of everything of the Earth. All crystal forms are variations of
these creative forms of the cosmic currents.

If we keep this imagination, this picture, in mind when
we look at a crystal, we will more readily feel its spiritual presence and its liveliness. Here, then, we have a
concept that matches what can be perceived when we
look lovingly and carefully into a crystal. Our usual
concept is that a crystal is dead matter growing out
of the earth from the precipitation of chemicals. And
different chemicals produce different forms. When we
look at a crystal from the place of our hearts, we both
see and feel a form, and it is even possible to feelingly
see the meeting of the outer form with the creative
Cosmos, right there at the boundary of the crystal's
faces and the surrounding space.

Further, when we observe a crystal with a sense of it
being formed from the spiritual Cosmos, we will be on
the way to seeing it as a miniature world, a presence here
on Earth of the world of specific angelic beings: the
gods clothed now in the substance of silica, for example.

In order to sense a crystal in this way, we have to relin-
quish the usual sense of ourselves a bit. As long as we
remain confined to our usual self-awareness, the crystal will appear as an object in front of us; and when

we are then told this and that about the powers of crystals, we may experience something, but we are barred from an intimate meeting with the stone and its world. All we experience, then, are impressionistic moments of the stone's world. These impressionistic moments are what get cataloged in various compendia of crystal lore. For example, clear Quartz is described as having a high vibration and is an all-purpose crystal with clear energy, which can be programmed for any purpose. I took this description directly from a catalog of stones. The same catalog describes Chrysocolla as "said to emit feminine energies, grounding, healing and Life Force." And green-gold Apatite is described in the following way: "Balances the polarities—mental and emotional, male and female, activity and serenity, love and will—bringing forth a dynamic balance in which well-being is enhanced and strength of purpose is combined with peace of mind."[9]

These descriptions imply stones are a little like angels who are being sold on the auction block and we are being told how they can serve us. Such an approach to crystals and minerals can slide into an attempt to control the spiritual worlds, as if we could get them to give us what we want. It is not that there is the absence of some truth in such descriptions. It is more that the descriptions do not go far enough. A much more sustained befriending of a crystal is needed in order to see it for what it is.

The kinds of descriptions given in New Age manuals of rocks reveal that there is a spectator-like distance between the observer and the crystal. Spectator consciousness bears the curse of remaining always on the surface of things. What we see through this kind of consciousness excludes the possibility of seeing and being united with the mineral or crystal in an act of love. Rather, what we see is pushed away from us through our object-consciousness and becomes an "outside thing" in front of us. The outer picture that our sense-perception gives us is disconnected from the angelic reality that is with us.

In order to break through our usual consciousness, which makes what it is present into an "object," it is necessary to understand that when we are developing the capacity to be *with* rather than *in front of* a crystal, we are developing the spiritual capacities of our sensing. We do so by developing our capacities of will and desire, because it is the unconscious acts of the will and of desire that keep us separate from what we experience. The two most basic necessities to come into the presence of the stone world are the acts of awakening consciously to sensing by loosening the hold cognition has on categorizing our sensing for us, and surrendering the will. The first, awakening sensing, comes about through quieting the mind and perceiving with the heart. Surrendering of the will cannot happen in a direct way. We cannot decide to surrender our will and then will ourselves to do so. Instead, surrender comes about by developing the capacity of *spiritual sensing* of the mineral worlds. Only through sensing can we see a stone's spiritual self.

There is a difference between "looking at" and "seeing." The great poet and artist William Blake said, "we do not see *with* the eye but rather *through* the eye." Seeing "with" the eye is soulless perceiving, when we are not within our seeing as the spiritual/soul beings that we are. Seeing *through* the eye means that there is an inner light: the eye is transparent, rather than just a bit of matter receiving stimuli from the environment that is then passed on to the brain where "seeing" takes place. Something—our life force, our soul-being, our spiritual individuality—goes out through this transparency and meets what we are looking at, and we begin to really see it.

There is a deep connection between the transparency of the eye and the transparency of stones.[10] Just as the transparency of the eye allows us to enter into an ensouled world and experience that world not as a world of surfaces "over there" but as a vast interiority with whom we are intimately connected, the transparency of a crystal connects us with the deepest spiritual interiority of the Cosmos as it is given to us in the appearance of a crystal.

Crystals are also sense organs. A clear, transparent Quartz crystal is the sense organ of the angelic beings whose currents have gathered from the vast Cosmos into this crystal. Just as with the human eye, for us to see soulfully we have to live within a sense of seeing as the transparency through which our soul/spirit light shines into the world. So too, the transparency of a crystal is its "seeing," its consciousness—its being *within* the spiritual worlds with which it is intimately connected and, through this transparency, letting the spiritual worlds shine within our souls.

But the crystal cannot see nor find its home without our help. Through our spiritual/soul seeing of the crystal, not only do we—to a greater or lesser degree—unite with the soul/spirit being that is the crystal, we occasion something far more significant. Through our intimate connection with the crystal, we are helping the beings of the crystal reunite with the spiritual Cosmos, and in that uniting, we help prepare the way for a "New Heaven and a New Earth."

In a way, crystals are exiled from their true home, the spiritual Cosmos. I say "in a way" because it is not complete separation; if it were, we would feel nothing from crystals. But crystals are not here for our benefit alone. They are here as a kind of potent residue of the spiritual worlds that are still active, and they are here for us to take them up in spiritual practices that can bring about a new spiritualizing, not only of the Cosmos, but of the Earth. This process occurs through our behaving like helpful spiritual beings rendering service to other spiritual beings—in this case, the spiritual presences of crystals and minerals.

Such a notion—the spiritualizing of the Earth through being present with the spiritual beings of the stone world—is spoken of quite explicitly in the Book of Revelations:

Immediately I was taken hold of by the spirit. And behold, a throne stood in Heaven, and Someone was sitting on it. And the One sitting on it was like Jasper and Sard to behold; and a rainbow stood above the throne and in it sat twenty-four elders, they wore white robes and had golden crowns on their heads. And lightning, voices, and thunder went forth from the throne; and before the throne were burning seven bright torches, which are the seven spirits of God. And before the throne it was like a sea of glass, like unto a crystal. . . . *(Emphasis added.)*

————————

The passage depicts the spiritual world. And at the same time, there is present in the spiritual world this "sea of glass, like unto a crystal." The passage is indicating that the spiritual world (the throne in heaven) and the earthly world (the sea of glass, like unto a crystal) will someday be one. That day can only come about through our spiritual efforts, the efforts of complete radical receptivity. The first movement on our part toward contributing to this unity of spiritual and earthly worlds is to develop the capacity to see the transparency of a crystal as a kind of consciousness.

Do not take transparency in a completely literal way. While a clear, transparent crystal is exemplar of transparency, every stone, even the most dense, has a soul quality of "transparency." Every stone is a medium, through which a connection and an exchange occurs between Earth and levels of the spiritual worlds. Just as a "medium" may be, for example, a person through whom a spiritual presence finds a voice in the world, stones are a constant voicing of the spiritual worlds. The scientific view of transparency says that it comes about through the atoms in the crystal matrix being ordered in such a way that they cannot be seen. The spiritual understanding says that the transparency of a crystal is evidence that the Earth is in unity with the spiritual worlds, in advance of our general recognition of this truth, and that the spiritual worlds are consciousnesses. That is, the transparency of a crystal is its mode of spiritual consciousness. The crystal's transparency is an emblem, an icon of the transparency, we might say—the invisibility of the spiritual world, as present here, though in a frozen state. Indeed, the meaning of the word "crystal" is "frozen water." The "water" referred to, though, is the complete fluidity of the spiritual world, the "sea of glass." When we enter the water through our soulful seeing and presence with a clear crystal, we enter into the purity of spiritual consciousness. This spiritual consciousness is not ours; it does not belong to us nor is it but tangentially connected to our personalities. The consciousness belongs to the spiritual beings, the angelic beings of the crystals.

A water-clear Quartz crystal, then, is pure, objectless, a spiritual consciousness within the earthly world. Thus transparent Quartz is a primary connector with the spiritual worlds. It is like a bridge between our usual sensing and a spiritual sensing of the spiritual worlds. It is for this reason that Quartz is so completely open to any interpretation that we give it. It is the earthly representative of the All. New Age descriptions of Quartz make this universal spirit consciousness in its earthly presence into multiple literal possibilities of the stone. These descriptions put forth the notion that we can use Quartz to program anything we want. What is lost, though, by telling us how to use clear Quartz for whatever we want, is that when clear Quartz is used as a metaphor for programming, we lose the sense of its spiritual Whole and instead go on the lookout for specific programmable qualities. In such a narrowing, we become forgetful of the Wholeness of the spiritual realms that constitute the crystal-worlds, and reduce these worlds to a device that gives us some specific thing that we want or think we need. More significantly, in using Quartz-consciousness for anything we want to program into it, we lose the capacity of being present to and within Wholeness. Wholeness becomes a mere abstraction, a theoretical idea, rather than an actual experience, wordless but infinitely profound. We miss the spiritual teaching of Quartz, as well as the potential for our selves to enter into complete transparency of spirit.

Stone transparency is consciousness. We cannot say, however, that when a crystal is less transparent, or is opaque, that opacity indicates an absence of consciousness. It does not even indicate a lesser degree of consciousness. Quartz is the connector consciousness between spiritual earth and spiritual Cosmos. It is like a clear conduit between realms. In itself it is clear of any forms except the form of connection between the worlds. There is more of the Earth with a cloudy or opaque stone; but this "more" is the more of the soul-Earth and the spirit-Earth. With more opaque stones, we are given more to do, in a spiritual sense. We have to enter into the opacity meditatively, receptively, and then let that opacity open to a transparency that will take us into the spiritual world of the stone. Specific ways of doing this will be described later.

A transparent stone does not demand quite the same act of the receptive will. More of the spiritual work is already done for us, so to speak. We can readily feel this difference by lovingly and contemplatively giving full attention to a water-clear Quartz crystal for several minutes, and then closing our eyes and feeling the inner calmness and even transparency of the luminous dark-ness we are within. Take an opaque stone and do the same meditative practice. When you close your eyes and feel the soul-presence of the opaque stone, there is still calmness, but there is also an inner sense of the dynamic movement of the opaqueness, which is felt interiorly like the movement of the stone-as-color. There is not literal movement, of course. You can nonetheless inwardly experience a felt sense of holding something dynamic. Inwardly, you no longer see the color; the color can nonetheless be felt as a kind of inward pull, a bit of a condensation, and if you allow your imagination its true freedom, it senses movement. You may feel that it is just your fantasy, but go with it: trust the felt sense. The clear Quartz is pure interior Light, pure spirit, held within the matter of the stone. Opaque stones have more *soul* qualities—that is what color is about, as we will see in a moment. (Opaque stones have more of a soul-spirit nature than does, say, clear Quartz; it is actually the Diamond that is the most spiritual of all the stones.)

Working with opaque stones develops the spiritual will, and may be of more spiritual value than working with transparent stones. I say "more valuable" because in working with opaque stones or translucent stones, we are also engaged in connecting with and purifying our soul lives, as well as working with the spirit realms. There is more inner work involved in entering into the felt spiritual presence of opaque stones. With opaque stones we are also working toward entering into the soul-dimensions of the Earth, whereas with transparent stones more of the spirit dimensions of the Cosmos reveal themselves. The distinction, however, is not absolute and is suggested only as an aid to orientation. In our inner work with opaque stones, it is as if we, through our inner images, transform an opaque stone into a transparent stone, and in so doing we are able to more readily be within the spiritual dimension of the stone. As we will see, this "spiritu-alizing" of opaque stones requires more will forces, but they are will forces free of entanglement with desire, as pointed out earlier.

Having, say, a Quartz crystal or any other mineral we want to work with, but now thinking of the stones as angelic beings rather than energies, is not sufficient if we have not changed our whole consciousness. If we do not experience an inner transfiguring of our very being based on perception, we are only substituting one word, "angels," for another word, "energies." I will speak in a moment about the meditative difference this change in orientation makes. For now, though, it is important to realize that if we have, say, a water-clear Quartz crys-tal, it is not as if we have an angelic being at our dis-posal, doing our bidding—which is a bit the way the programming metaphor sets it up. It is also not as if each specimen of the mineral world is an angel in dis-guise. All of the crystals, minerals, or stones of a given class are resonating presences of a particular realm of angelic beings. Think of all the Quartz of the Earth as all-connected, a whole being—something like a bee-hive. The analogy has a lot to it. Just as the beehive is one whole, consisting of multiple cells—which are, interestingly, six-sided structures just like Quartz crystals—all of the Quartz of the world is one whole with multiple cells, which are the individual Quartz crystals. Similarly, all the Tourmaline is the Earth-presence of a whole spiritual being, as are all the other crystals and minerals.

The seven crystal systems (cubic, hexagonal, trigonal, tetragonal, rhombic, monoclinic, and triclinic) are the particular forms that resonate in different spiritual realms. Thus, when we hold a crystal, part of the befriending of the crystal-as-being is to notice its form, notice the way that the Light of the All incarnates in particular and differing ways.

When we notice not just in an external way, but by taking into our interior soul the form of the mineral we feel drawn to work and be with, our souls are changed. Our souls become greater and more comprehensive: they begin to be able to recognize as feeling, not as a mental concept, the different beings at work in each crystal system.

One not need conceptually know all the crystal systems. The cubic form of Pyrite, for example, conveys a feeling of solidity, while the hexagonal form of the Quartz crystal has the quality of a "reaching out," a gathering of the Cosmos-as-a-whole within the Quartz in such a way that the spiritual Quartz-world reflects upon itself while at the same time holding nothing for itself. This is a felt quality. Working with crystals helps us become much more aware of the subtlety and specificity of the capacities of our own souls. All this is bypassed when careful, loving, particular perceptual attention toward the mineral is bypassed. Rudolf Steiner indicates:

... then we see the mineral realm, which by its nature contains crystals. Crystals, mineral crystals, become wonderful objects of research and observation precisely for the person seeking entry into the spiritual worlds. Once again, one feels compelled to lift one's gaze from the crystallized minerals one encounters on earth to the world—all, to the cosmos. ... Once again one experiences the essence of things out there in the cosmos, and once more one says to oneself: what we experience down here as crystallized minerals is caused by the living spirit found in the expanse of the cosmos.[11]

In addition to transparency and form, crystals and minerals are also characterized by color. Notice what happens with when we lovingly, carefully, notice the color of a stone. Something quite different happens than when we notice the transparency or the form. The water-clear Quartz is united with us in consciousness as a "reaching toward" the spiritual worlds and as "receiving-from" the spiritual worlds—it contains both qualities at the same time. The color of a stone, when united with our consciousness, is not the resonating presence of the angelic beings alone or of the spiritual Cosmos, but rather is also the resonating presence of the soul and of the spiritual qualities of the Earth. The felt-sense of the color, something related to but beyond the reaction of awe we might have to the beauty of the color, is something like, "Ah, here this spiritual presence of the beings of the Cosmos clothes itself with the soul-substance of this world, with color." And color is never neutral; the soul absorbs color, feels and enjoys the qualities of color. Color is like a more-earthly cloak worn by a spiritual being—but the cloak is of a soul-spiritual nature. There are earthly soul-spiritual presences as well as cosmic spiritual presences; and they perfectly unite in crystals and minerals with color. Color arises from a mixture of light and darkness; the Light of the spiritual world must be combined with the spiritual coloring of the Earth for there to be the colors of stones we experience. At one time, when the world was more spiritually oriented than it is today, there was an understanding of the color of stones that is closer to the one given here. In his *Book of Nature*, written in 1482, Konrad von Megenberg wrote: "The coloration of stones, which, black, green, red, violet, and so forth, arises through the influence of heavenly bodies on the changing ratio between gases and moisture."[12] It is a nice expression of the interplay of cosmic spiritual beings and earthly soul-spiritual beings—provided we realize that gas and moisture are the expressions of elemental beings.

Today, science tells us that the colors of crystals come from the presence of traces of metals within the chemical composition of the stone. It is true that the color of crystals and minerals comes from traces of metals. These colors are, so to speak, drawn out of the Earth by the planets. The planets have always been esoterically recognized as the presence of soul-beings in the Cosmos; the stars and the constellations have always been recognized as the presence of spiritual beings within the Cosmos.

The planets have also always been esoterically connected with the metals. For example:

Mercury—Quicksilver

Venus—Copper

Jupiter—Tin

Saturn—Lead

Mars—Iron

Moon—Silver

Sun—Gold

Minerals and crystals with these elements are colored by both the cosmic realms and the earthly realms simultaneously. There are many other metals that have other cosmic resonances such as aluminum, indium, gallium, thallium, lithium, sodium, potassium, and beryllium. Perhaps these are the resonances of the outer planets—and even of unknown planets. The planetary forces draw out the metals from within the Earth. These metals, in their soul-action rather than through their chemical composition, bring soul qualities into crystals and minerals.

Without color, we would be taken into the spiritual Cosmos in working with crystals but would lose the sense of the soul, of the delicious sense of interiority and warmth, and of connectedness to the Earth as a soul as well as a spirit being. The color of stones is experienced by us as a felt sense of "inwardness," and in different ways depending on the colors of the stone.

Our delight in stones is often related to their colors. Notice that the color often has a kind of "otherworldly" character to it. The colors of minerals are not like objects which are painted on the surface. There is an indescribable depth to the color of stones; the otherworldly sense of a depth that has been illuminated by the heights. With the deep blue of Azurite, for example, we have darkness coming into the light. Such color produces an inward sense of comfort, a bodily knowing that we will not be swallowed by the darkness. The red color of Rhodonite conveys a sense of the realm of light entering the realm of darkness. The inward sense of this color is a bodily felt comfort that we will not be dissolved into the Light. These kinds of qualities are the way the spiritual qualities of stones speak to us.

Colors are thus the souls of the stones. There is a radical difference, though, between the souls of stones and the souls of human beings. The stone's soul is characterized by Silence beyond Silence, complete purity, and complete absence of desire. By purity, I mean that a stone is not pulled in any way into confusion about itself. Nor does a stone convey, even in a stone-sense, that it is pulled toward being anything other than that which it is. It is color that draws us into intimacy with stones, and when we feel at ease and at rest with a stone—when we enter so deeply into the stone that we go deeply, deeply into Silence and into feeling the color quality of the stone—then the stone is a helping partner in the purification of our own soul. Purity constitutes, in addition to Silence, one of the primary spirit/soul characteristics of the mineral world. According to Steiner:

The human being is still permeated with urges and desires, with passions. Our physical nature is imbued with all this. But there is an ideal that stands before us; the animal nature of the human being will gradually be purified to a level at which the human body will be present to us every bit as chastely and free of wishes as the mineral, which desires nothing, in which no wish stirs if anything comes near it. Chaste and pure is the inner material nature of the mineral. This chasteness and purity are the feelings with which we should be imbued in the presence of the mineral world. Each feeling of this kind is specific to the individual forms and colors displayed by the mineral world; but the fundamental feeling that fills the mineral world is chasteness.[13]

We must not think of the mineral world as being free of desire; that is not what purity means. Purity means first that desire is rightly directed, and second, that it is not confused with other forms and kinds of desire. Pure desire is our longing for the Divine and the Divine's longing for us. Minerals, I think, live constantly, without wavering, in this sense of desire. Spiritual work with the mineral world is thus primarily the spiritual path of desire, desire without attachment to an object. By working spiritually with the mineral world, our bodies undergo a transfiguration in which our own desires become clarified, purified, and transformed into longing for the Divine (which is also a connection with the Divine). It is, however, the combination of the soul element of color and the spiritual aspects of the stone together that makes a stone a holy presence, through which we can develop spiritually. That is, the stone's color, transparency, and form are harmoniously united.

When we hold a crystal or a mineral, our orientation toward it changes dramatically if we feel this constant meeting of worlds—the spiritual Cosmos and the spiritual Earth. Then we do not get caught and confused, changing our metaphors of stones or going back and forth between imagining stones in relation to spiritual beings in one moment and thinking of them as chemical, metal, dead matter the next. The result of such confusion is that our own souls cannot develop their capacities of being with the stone realm in a consistent spiritual way. Without this strengthening of our souls, we cannot begin working with stones in ways that are for the sake of the spiritual worlds first, and only indirectly but surely also for the healing of humanity and individuals.

Contemplative Practice I
Entering the Silence and Befriending a Stone

How do you enter into the Silence of a stone? It is imperative to hold and look at the stone—a lot. Small chips of stone can work, but it is better to have a good-sized stone. Let the stone be in your vicinity—around where you work. Let it get a feeling for you, though what its "feelings" are like is hard to say. I do know that having a stone I am called to work with changes it, and it changes me, provided that I notice it from time to time.

It helps a great deal to gaze at the stone with your attention in the center of your heart. At the time one does this, nothing may seem to happen. But often, after treating a stone in this manner, you may find that it is as if the stone comes alive. It begins to radiate a kind of inner light, and the very distinct feeling is present that this indeed is a precious, sacred presence. You may find your eye taken into the translucency of a red stone as light shines from within it. Let your gaze wander where it wants to; the stone will be the guide. On one thin plate of Chalcedony that rests before me, for example, my eye is taken over the sparkling carpet of twinkling star-like lights. Then, looking at the stone from the side, light and dark blue-gray wavy bands unfurl along the edge. And the other side of the stone is a dark, red-brown matrix that appears as if it is coming from the deepest part of the Earth. Here, with this small stone, the range of experience from the starry heavens to the underworld is all present, at once. And, surprisingly, when you go back to the stone from time to time, to a stone that you have had a long time, and each time it is approached from the heart, in the depth of Silence, you will find you are taken into it as if for the first time. This practice alone suffices as a profound entry practice into the spiritual world of stones. From our initial getting to know a stone on its own terms, we proceed on the Stone Path by giving complete and focused sensory attention to a stone. Think of the stone you are working with as a sacred object and contemplate how to rightly come into the presence of a sacred object. Approach it with calmness, entering first into a feeling of the Sacred Silence that surrounds and permeates the stone. Enter the Silence before working with the stone. Simply sit quietly, with eyes closed, holding the stone, entering into a bodily state of radical receptivity. At this point, you are not focusing your mind on anything; rather, let your attention—your attention, not your thinking— be present to your own bodily form and feel the Silence permeating your body. Entering the Silence is a step beyond relaxation—more active noticing than relaxation, but still receptive.

There will be a moment when you will notice a felt-sense of your body uniting with the "field" surrounding it—a kind of feeling that the space around you is active and living, a holy presence. There is a feeling of a permeability of your body and the surrounding space. You are completely alert, not in a trance state.

Begin gazing at the stone with your attention centered in your heart and, at the same time, within the stone. Begin to lovingly and carefully notice the characteristics of the stone. Your attention will be attracted to certain things: for example, a small rainbow in a crystal, a flicker of colored light when the stone is held a certain way, the sheen, the depth of the color, the transparency, the beauty of the form, or the complete strangeness of what you are seeing. As you notice each characteristic—more through the feeling that comes than by the intellect inventorying qualities—take that sensory quality inward into your heart. One by one, take each quality noticed into the heart. What is seen in a sensory way then becomes present as interior feeling. We are trying to circumvent the intellect—not to get rid of it, but to allow it to move into the background and let the heart feeling come to the fore.

You will notice a particular moment when you feel a sense of wonder and awe: that is the moment the intellect has relinquished its treasured place of having to know. You find that you are in deep and intimate relationship with the stone. It is no longer simply an object. Feel its holiness. The inner work is to simply be present with and within this awe without searching for anything.

This practice can be done with many stones. It is a wonderful way of developing a capacity of wonder and love in relation with a stone. Through such a practice, begin to develop an intuitive sense of the more subtle qualities of the stone—what it does, at what level it affects you the most. Most importantly, you will begin to find your orientation shift from wanting something to happen, to experiencing an inner joy at simply being with the stone.

The stone changes too by being noticed in this way. It is now a presence. Sometimes, quite often, after engaging a stone in this manner the changes are quite dramatic. The color may intensify, or spread more through the stone. I have had stones that begin to grow small crystals on them. Another stone has changed dramatically in color. A subtle quality of softness emanates from the stone. You will feel now, every time you see the stone, that you want to look at it and be engaged with it in this way.

Work with the stone in this sensory way before sleep. Be aware of how the presence of the stone lingers in your imagination; images of the stone may even appear inwardly. When you wake in the morning, be aware of what come first into awareness: the memory of a dream, a thought, the presence of a feeling, bodily sensations, or a way the light appears on the wall. Whatever you notice, no matter how small or seemingly insignificant, this first awareness is the stone's response to your attention to it. What comes to awareness upon waking may seem to have nothing to do with the stone. Our usual consciousness is used to functioning in a cause/effect or a before/after fashion, with the intellect making a presumed connection. Consciousness that functions according to the laws of Wholeness does not seek a response that is so logically connected to the stone's sensory presence.

This kind of sensing is the most important step in working spiritually with stones. It clears all unconscious preconceptions one might have and not even be aware of. It develops the capacity of sensory empathy, the ability to be completely with something through the senses without any intervening concept. It prepares us for the next contemplative step of the Stone Path.

CHAPTER 3

Stones and the Circulation of Gifts

Where do all the characteristics and gifts that books list stones as providing come from? Awakening of chakras, healing, a clear sense of destiny, heart-feeling, courage, stronger will forces, alignment, clear communication, heart health, protection from danger, connecting with nature spirits, calming the emotional body, activation of clairvoyant abilities—the list is endless. And, more importantly, are all the qualities that emanate from stones really wholly for us and our use? There may be more possibilities than using stones for our personal and spiritual gain. The way of working with stones that I am describing, at least, leads us to something more expansive than that. And that "more" begins with lovingly befriending each stone. Part of befriending involves continually noticing different experiences we might have with a stone, for a stone does not reveal itself all at once.

A second part of this way of working with crystals and minerals focuses on re-visioning all of the gifts stones are said to provide, and finding a way of returning those gifts to where they came from in the first place. What we then receive from crystals and minerals may be more subtle than imagined up to this point by stone workers.

I am going to be using the term "crystallized" more than once in this section. I am not referring to crystals only, but to the entire process of mineralization as it has occurred in the evolution of the Earth. The Whole of the spiritual Cosmos crystallizes into the forms of the mineral world in the course of Earth's evolution, which is still going on. This means that particular spiritual presences of the Cosmos, through the sacrifices they made to form the Earth, are in a way frozen—solidified into the objects we know as crystals, minerals, and stones. This crystallization process goes the furthest with aggregate stones, those stones consisting of a conglomeration of minerals that are not uniform in the way in which minerals and crystals are. With aggregate stones, there is a predominance of earth forces and a near absence of cosmic, spiritual forces in the formation of the stone. With crystals and minerals, there is more of a uniformity of particular spiritual presences.

The crystallization process, however, is never complete. Something of the active, living spiritual currents remain. You can see these active currents by gazing at a stone until you see its aura. For example, I have a small, white, sparkling Azeztulite. When I place this mineral on a white piece of paper and gaze in a diffuse way at the stone by looking at the periphery of the stone and beyond, rather than directly focusing on it, a purple/blue aura can be seen emanating around the edges of the stone. This aura is similar to the human aura in that the aura around the human body also indicates that the body is more expansive than the physical form we see; the body, too, has not completely crystallized into an only-physical thing.

The way in which spiritual beings resonate within crystals and minerals involves an intermediate step in the relation between the cosmic spiritual forces from which crystals and minerals originate and the presence of crystals and minerals within Earth. The creative beings of crystals and minerals do not directly enter into the earthly mineral realm. The angelic beings of crystals and minerals work through intermediaries—elemental beings, who both carry the crystallization process and keep the living currents active in the solid element. In the esoteric tradition, when elemental beings are caught in a crystallizing process it is called "enchantment."

We owe everything around us to the creative spiritual beings and to their intermediaries, the Elementals. The "surplus" of forces, the indirectly felt presence of the creative angelic beings of the mineral worlds, is readily experienced by those who develop even a modicum of body-consciousness. It is this surplus of the creative forces of the angelic beings, working through the elemental beings, that is described in all the metaphysical crystal and mineral books as doing all of those things that we want for ourselves.

The real work soon becomes more clear. Through being with crystals and minerals—sensing them as described, holding them, emptying our minds, entering into Silence, and placing our attention into our hearts—we gradually increase the sensitivity of the body so that the currents can be felt much more strongly.

That we bodily feel something—a current, sometimes a kind of "tingling," maybe a wave of feeling—when we hold certain crystals or minerals indicates that an initial encounter between the enchanted elemental being and us has occurred. And through that relating, that announcement of a presence, there is a further encounter between the creative angelic being's resonance in the stone and us.

It may well be that the initial currents we feel from stones, which are often somewhat uncomfortable, are the pains of the trapped elemental beings. Books of stones describe these strong currents as having to do with energy intensities that our body may not be familiar with, and advise holding or wearing the stone for short periods of time until we become used to the higher and more intense frequencies. The unpleasantness of the currents can also be quieted by inwardly acknowledging that more expansive currents of the stone are meeting with a more contracted bodily vibration. Surely, the unpleasant feeling is a lowering rather than a raising and an expansion of bodily vibration. We can resolve the discomfort by inwardly shifting our own bodily vibration, moving it in an upward and expansive direction by our intent. The discomfort will cease, which also indicates that the elemental being's constrained frequency is also being adjusted by our intent. This is our first service to the mineral world, and one which opens our body to the spiritual presence of the angelic beings of stones.

If we take the bodily sensations in their initial discomfort as something to become accustomed to, it is likely that we become numb to the currents and at the same time become open to suggestion and fantasy, which gives us the illusory sense that what we are experiencing emanates from the stones themselves. The initial gesture from the stone must be met with more than our first caring attention. We have invited the stone into us rather than adjusting our body downward, which would only increase our own egotistic tendencies. On the other hand, when we adjust our bodily response toward the stone, we have made an important step in getting beyond a smaller self.

A further step concerns releasing the long list of desires for a stone to do something specific for us that we have when purchasing or finding a stone. The "diviners" of crystals and minerals tell us, "this stone will open our crown chakra," "this one will strengthen our heart forces," "this one will open our feelings and allow us to be more vulnerable," "this stone will help with diabetes, this one with vision," or "these stones will initiate us into immortality." When inundated with information like this, the psyche absorbs it and it then lives within us unconsciously, becoming a source of suggestion, fantasy, and projection. This inevitability is no different than anything that is offered of a soul or a spiritual nature as being of help. In all such subtle areas, it is necessary to develop discipline and practices that assure we are in connection with the spiritual dimension.

The "diviners" themselves come to these qualities through working meditatively with the stones. It is, for them, a matter of developing intuition to a certain point. Intuition is a high level of feeling. It is not mentally cognitive, it is not a thinking "about" the stone; it is a mode of being within the living presence of the stone. What is not considered, however, is that perhaps these intuited qualities do not only belong to the beings of the stone. Perhaps stones are not "giving" these qualities to us at all—or at least that possibility is far from all that is truly going on. The moment we feel that stones are giving us certain qualities in a direct way, that is an indication that the vibrational frequency of the stone has been moved in a downward direction and whatever is being offered is now mixed with our own desires. For now we have transferred a spiritual quality of a stone into a purely human meaning. We have stepped down the stone's frequency, and in so doing have begun to make it speak our language. This is the opposite direction of allowing the stones to transfigure our being and entering into modes of experience that are completely unfamiliar to us and which cannot be reduced to human meaning. The direction we seek is that of going into completely different worlds and inwardly following where those worlds take us.

To expect that having a particular crystal or mineral will result in increasing one of the particular attributes of the stone for us, or to work with it without entering the work of the path of stones, may well be short-circuiting a much larger process than we who are interested in crystals and minerals are called to—now, in this time, at this particular moment in the spiritual evolution of the Earth, the Cosmos, and Humanity. Hearing these attributes, being attracted to those "gifts of the stone," may also be a first introduction to a unique spiritual path. On this path, the desire to obtain these attributes for oneself has to be sacrificed, inwardly given away, again and again—for the sake of the angelic beings of the stones, for the sake of the spiritualizing of the Earth, and for the spiritualizing of the human being. Here, we are asked to admit that we do not know what is going on, that the spiritual worlds have their own intention, and that stones are spiritual teachers rather than servants of our desires—no matter how noble the desires might seem.

There is a long and wonderful tradition of the kind of compendia of crystals and minerals we now have. For example, a very interesting one is *De Virtutibus Lapidum (The Virtues of Stones)* by Damigeron, dating from the second century BC. It may be the oldest lapidary in the West. The descriptions of stones in this book are much like the compendia of our day, expressing, however, the desires and needs of the people of those times. Here is an example:

Selenite. The stone Selenite is like Jasper. It is a strong, heavy, bright, wonderful, blessed stone. Its brightness increases as the moon waxes and decreases as it wanes. It is useful for many things. It is good for love and lawsuits. Tie to those who are weak with tuberculosis when the moon is waxing; or even if we do it on the contrary when it is waning, it does wonders.[14]

Now, here are excerpts of the same stone given in Robert Simmons's book, *The Book of Stones:*

Selenite quickly opens and activates the third eye, crown chakra, and the Soul Star chakra above the head.... Selenite is fast and effective at cleansing the auric field, and it can clear congested energies or negativity from one's physical and etheric body.... Placing a Selenite wand upon one's back, along the length of the spine, one can achieve an energetic alignment of the vertebrae and the chakras as well.... Selenite can lift one's awareness to higher planes of inner experience, making it possible for one to consciously meet one's spirit guides and guardian angels.[15]

There is little correspondence between the virtues of the stone as described by these authors separated by centuries in their writing. But the genre is very similar:

both are concerned with what stones can give us and stones are taken as devices that either provide instant physical attributes or instant spiritual attributes. *The present evolutionary moment, however, is very different.* From the time of the first description above until now, the locus of the actions of crystals and minerals on humans has changed. The more recent part of the evolution of consciousness has been the very gradual development of the capacity to utilize individuality to turn toward unification with the spiritual worlds. The descriptions from these two books show the basic differences in orientation—in terms of desires. The first description helps in purely earthly matters; the second clearly shows a different orientation, one of coming closer to spiritual desires. Both, however, hold to the assumption that the spiritual worlds—in the form of stones—are here for our benefit. At this time, we are in the midst of a further aspect of spiritual evolution. The development of the capacity to utilize individual freedom allows us not only to turn toward the spiritual worlds, but to enter fully into becoming spiritual human beings—not simply human beings who do spiritual things and have spiritual aspirations. Now is the time when we can freely participate in spiritualizing not only our own being, but also the being of Earth. A crucial aspect of this development concerns the way we work with the mineral kingdom to aid in releasing the enchanted beings of stones to be returned to the spiritual Cosmos. Those forces, when released, will further the spiritual unfolding of the Earth.

Humans are also a part of that further spiritual unfolding—and we can get a sense of the nature of that unfolding by re-visioning the gifts of crystals and minerals. The primary purpose of the "spiritual path of stones" is to develop a spiritual circulation between the earthly realms and the spiritual realms without assuming that we know what the angelic beings of the stones will bring to us.

We are at a critical spiritual evolutionary moment of the Earth and of Humanity. We are being invited to develop spiritual capacities in order to become partners, spiritual coworkers with the beings of crystals and minerals. A first aspect of this work is not to simply let the elemental and angelic beings that resonate within stones wander inside us as a result of our fascination with their beauty, but rather to aid in the restoration of Wholeness from the ground up.

By means of our soul and spirit activity working together with that of the stones, we free the enchanted elemental beings of the stones and come into more direct connection with the creative angelic beings of the stones. In this process we become more spiritually conscious and experience healing from the creative beings of the stones. The nature of this healing, though, is different than the point-to-point kind of healing that is now expected from crystals. By "point-to-point" I mean we expect one crystal to heal one form of ailment, another kind of crystal to do something else, and so on. This way of viewing healing is a result of the medicalization of healing. True healing always proceeds from immersion in the Whole; it is not an empirical point-to-point process. This difference will be clarified further on in this and the next section.

The characteristic "gifts" that are attributed to crystals and minerals are first and foremost the inwardness of the stones—that is, their gifts, not their gifts *to us*. If a child has a gift of playing the piano, that is the child's gift, not ours. What we receive from the child's gift is often filled with wonder and surprise. It is no different with minerals and crystals. While a stone's form, hardness, and color, are outward gestures of its consciousness, what the compendia say stones give to us are in fact what belongs to the stones as their attributes. We could even say their attributes are dimension of the stones' consciousnesses. When someone tells us that they have the gift of a certain characteristic—say, courage—their telling us so does not thereby imbue us with that characteristic. Why, then, do we expect that intuiting the qualities of crystals and minerals automatically imbues us with those virtues? It is much more sensible to realize that we may be, at the level of our soul and at the level of our spirit, introduced by stones to qualities that we know absolutely nothing about, qualities we have no concepts for. We are thus required to enter into being transfigured by the spiritual-mineral worlds rather than being informed about what they can do for us.

The process of feeling currents from stones, being inwardly moved by those currents, and assuming that we are receiving what the compendia of stones indicate, sounds more like a process of being cured by suggestion. We are all too ready to accept half-truths for whole truths. For example, if we feel the Selenite currents as described by a book of stones, we feel what we have read about: we automatically assume that a third-eye awakening is happening, that our aura is cleansed, or that we are having an encounter with our guardian angel. These are all known spiritual notions, and thus constitute, at the most, "add-ons" to who we are rather than the truer but far more radical truth: uniting with stone consciousness completely reconfigures our soul, spirit, body—even our physiological being.

In our infinite cleverness, stones will also be found that are said to reconfigure us in such radical ways too.

The trouble is, such attributes of stones (undoubtedly "newly discovered") are not actually transfiguring our being, but rather, at the most, changing our mentality concerning who we think we are as human beings. We then have momentary experiences of qualities we may not have experienced before, or maybe even strong bodily experiences. Are we actually undergoing a transfiguration of our being?

To say, for example, that the stone Morganite "opens the heart to love, releases old pain, brings a sense of peace and joy, confidence and power, and a connection with Divine love; that it cleanses and energizes the heart and emotional body, heals fear, resentment and anger; that it clears old difficult relationships, and helps one attune to the energy of abundance"[16] takes a intuitive connection with the elemental and creative angelic presence resonating within Morganite and translates this intuition into something that the stone does for us. It translates intuition into understandable mental notions.

Morganite, in fact, is probably connected with angelic beings that are the creative beings of these kinds of qualities—*but not as we know these qualities according to our concepts of these qualities.* The alteration of our being in the Morganite direction, for example, would have to do with entirely new seed qualities, of which these known concepts are paltry expressions. These expressions can actually keep us tied to who we already are, instead of open us to what we can become as new human beings. We can add on heart, love, peace, joy, confidence, power, etc. to who we are. We can have, through stones, certain kinds of spiritual experiences—which we may then attempt to have around more frequently. These kinds of spiritual experience are not initiatory; we have not gone through something that will be more than for our personal use. Goethe once said, "from the power that binds all beings, that man frees himself who overcomes himself." Spiritual work with stones is a primary way of finding our true selves by getting beyond our known selves.

The intuition given in books on stones is not wrong; but it cannot stay at that level without turning into an egotism of stones, that is, the attempt to magically use stones for our own purposes. The first movement deeper, one that is not at all difficult, is to carry the stone with us, return to it over and over, meditate with it, and—most importantly—begin to be inwardly aware of what our interior life is like with the presence of the stone.

It is wise to refrain from jumping to the meanings of the stone as given in the books. We will likely be infected by suggestion. To experience something by suggestion is not to say that what is experienced is incorrect; remaining at the level of suggestion means that we do not develop our own capacities of an active inner life able to meet the beings of stones on their own terms. We may be genuinely affected by the stone due to the suggestion, but the Stone Path requires inner work.

Close presence with a stone over time begins to be experienced inwardly as the felt presence of an unknown quality within us, which is also felt bodily. We feel visited. It is as if there is an autonomous presence within us. We begin to discover that the inner life too has its autonomy and is not all about "us"—like a second-self that is us and not us at the same time. Whereas in usual consciousness there is not a sense of the interior of our being because we identify completely with our physical being, this changes when we are more present to the action of a crystal or a mineral, not just at the time of meditating with them, but as we carry, hold, and return to them over and over again. We gradually discover ourselves as different—not just as having something we did not have before, but as different beings; structurally different, not just happier, healthier, feeling more alive, and more spiritual.

We lose something too. We lose the sense of ourselves as having been formed by the past, by what has happened to us. We also lose the sense of belonging to the collective world of mass consciousness and its pleasures, pains, hopes, and expectations. We lose the sense that there is something "outside" that will provide all we need—if we could only find it—or that some person, organization, or political party will solve the difficulties of the world and thus those difficulties as they touch us.

The recognition begins to dawn on us that the world as now given is all upside-down, that humanity is totally caught up in working for its own benefit and that when we are right-side up, we are intended to work continually for the sake of the spiritual worlds. Times where this rightness of direction was lived were times of remarkable cultures, such as the ancient Indian, Persian, Egyptian, and Greek cultures. Only now, however, at this time of the evolution of consciousness are we free to once again make such a culture. Such a spiritual culture can never be made by humanity alone, left to our own cleverness. We have to start from the ground up by giving to the spiritual worlds rather than receiving from them. Stones are our teachers of this new way.

The initial felt interiority that develops with a stone is not particularly comfortable. It is more like something within that is attempting to get our attention. At the same time, we experience a quality of "concaveness" within—as if we are giving interior space to and for the crystal; and this concaveness is filled with force. This force can be anywhere from a kind of irritation to a very pleasant and relaxing feeling or even a strong emotional feeling, depending on what stone we are working with. Neither feeling is simply to be endured, for what is being experienced is a vibratory action that is different than that of our body. The inward task is to "lift" the body's vibration to the level of the autonomous vibratory quality. This elevation of vibration can easily be accomplished by an intent to do so accompanied by a felt bodily empathy with the new vibration. It is a bodily process of "listening" to a "visitor." It can take some time and practice to know when this uniting of the body with the new vibration has occurred. An inner quality of light occurs as well as a shifting from the more emotional tenor of irritation or pleasantness into pure calmness.

A further elaboration of getting accustomed to the presence of the elemental and creative angelic beings of stones consists of a form of contemplation with them. The word "con-template" means "being within the temple." Indeed, when we work actively with crystals and minerals there is a sense that we have stepped into a holy temple. The act necessary in a temple is complete, open, radical receptivity. Receptivity, is not simply letting ourselves be taken over; it is something very active. In receptivity, we meet what comes into us, welcome those forces, become actively present to them, and yield to them without losing the sense of who we are, although the ego sense of who we think we are is suspended.

The fact that we experience bodily qualities when holding a stone means that the stone is being sensed; a sensory process is going on and the nerves are being stimulated. What we feel, though, when carrying, wearing, and being with the crystal in contemplation, is also the blood and the fluid processes of the body coming into harmony with the presence of the sensory processes. We are being spiritually "enlarged" when we give our attention to this subtle unfolding. The challenge is allowing this process to happen, tracking it, not interpreting it, and remaining open to what may unfold. It is a tremendous slowing down of what crystal lore usually presents.

The temporary irritation that often comes when holding a stone described as having high frequency vibrations simply means that we experience the stone through our nerves. In working with stones, we are not transformed by sensory nerve processes; their stimulation quickly reverts into our having thoughts about what is happening. Rudolf Steiner calls the blood and fluid processes the Life Processes. They are far deeper than sensory processes and more of the soul rather than the spirit dimension. The Life Processes are what undergo transfiguration on the spiritual path of stones.

Through this contemplative way of being with crystals and minerals, we are in the process of building a Body of Light. We can tell this is happening—it is something beyond New Age talk. As we continue our inner connection with stones, if we from time to time close our eyes and let our attention go toward the interior of our body, we will experience a luminous body of mist. It was there all along, but opening to the presence of the beings of crystals begins to intensify its activity so that it is much more readily felt and experienced. This Body of spiritual Light, then, becomes the primary mode of our interaction with elemental and creative angelic presences of crystals and minerals. We are not given a Body of Light by the mineral substances, and if we try to make use of crystals according to a literal reading of what books say, we will bypass this crucial discovery on the Stone Path. The Body of Light is built through the relationship of interiority between ourselves and the stones.

A NOTE ON THE BODY OF LIGHT

"The changing of bodies into light, and light into bodies, is very comfortable to the course of nature, which seems delighted with transmutation."

—Sir Isaac Newton

While there exists some writing on the Light Body, I take my description of it from the work of Rudolf Steiner in his book *From Jesus to Christ*.[17] While I had read this book long ago, at that time it was only of intellectual interest. Only after working with crystals and minerals in the way described thus far, and upon experiencing in an indirect way this body of Light, did I go back and read this work again. In the existent metaphysical literature, the Light Body is often taken to be something other than the physical body, and thus of a completely ethereal spiritual nature—a view that contributes to the general way in which spirituality is seen as a form of escapism from the Earth. Steiner does not take that approach. Yet he does not develop a theory of the Light Body either. What he says is based in his own clairvoyant research.

What we today call the "physical body" is for Steiner rightly called "the crystallized body." The actual physical body that is in union with the cosmic worlds is invisible. It is the Body of Light. The Body of Light is a form, a transparent network of spiritual forces that exists as a kind of spiritual vessel for the mineral forces and substances.

This transparent form—Steiner also calls it the "phantom body"—in the course of human evolution became buried in and disorganized by human actions. The body ceased to be the true Body—and the earth ceased to be the true Earth. Earth too is a Light Body, but it is one that will be developed only through our spiritual efforts, aided by the beings of crystals and minerals. The circulation between the Light Body and the spiritual Cosmos will gradually bring about a transformation of Earth into its light body, called "Terra Lucida" in the Sufi Tradition.

Steiner also says that the human body, the true physical body of light, consists of the perfectly transparent, crystal-clear "Philosopher's Stone":

"The truth is that the human being, in the course of Earth evolution, lost the form of the physical body, so that humankind no longer had what the divine beings intended from the beginning. It is something we must regain.[18]

Here we begin to sense the fuller significance of taking the spiritual path of stones. However, it is a path to be trod step by step—experientially. A view such as Steiner's can be a help, but it does not replace the needed effort of slow contemplative work accompanied by phenomenological description.

Releasing the desires that are connected with stones, and which are given in the many books as statements concerning what each particular stone is supposed to do, frees the qualities from their attachment to the unconscious. Thus, those qualities now become an invitation from the spiritual beings of the stones. For example, perhaps some books on stones say that having certain minerals around increases one's spiritual drive, makes one more extroverted, invigorates and livens, or helps one out of a state of apathy; makes one hopeful and optimistic; mobilizes energy reserves; improves posture and helps with problems of bones, cartilage, and joints. If we have any of these problems and we work with crystals, perhaps someone will direct us to this stone. Or we may feel an attraction to this stone. Its list of attributes, though, is a translation into human language of unknown characteristics of the spiritual beings of this variety of stone. Rather than naively taking what is said of a stone and purchasing the stone thinking that these qualities will magically enter into our personality, there is another way to work with such descriptions that yields attention to the stone's consciousness rather than to our desires.

It is very helpful to read the listing of stone qualities as a human translation of something coming from the stone. Given such a realization, the first step is to return what is given in such descriptions to the stones themselves. This stone, we could interpret, is a being of spiritual strength who has a radiating rather than concentrated Silence. It is a being whose spiritual structure itself exudes strength and the power of formation. This being lives within the human bodily structure as the spiritual forces within our bones, cartilage, and joints.

This kind of "hermeneutic"—that is, hearing words through occult listening and reading what is written as a description of our being as used by the stones—reorients us in a new direction: toward spiritual geography and geology rather than the direction of our usual understanding of what we are doing. We are quite foolish to assume there is a direct line from stones to us in which they give themselves to enhance all of the personality characteristics that keep us away from their spiritual beings in the first place. Such hubris belies ages of esoteric and spiritual work showing the kind of effort and sacrifice needed to have even a minimal sense of what the spiritual realms are like.

This reorientation is only a first step in allowing the soul of the stone to join our own soul lives. Before one moves further, a good deal of practice needs to be done with manuals of stones, engaging in this kind of reorientation to the point that it becomes impossible to look at a compendium of stones without hearing the descriptions as the stones' self-revelation—in their first aspect. It is good to take descriptions from two or three books, read them, and then let the words inwardly resonate until an inward "turning" is felt. This inward turning is the ego's identification with the soul releasing its hold. Until such a release can be felt, we are caught in our own desires. Thus, occult hearing is an act of purification of desire.

Here are some examples of this kind of hearing.

Carnelian—Compendium Description:

Book one: "Red Carnelian symbolizes activity. It promotes helpfulness and idealism and encourages community spirit. Carnelian works mainly on the sacral chakra. Carnelian is particularly effective for life in those born under Aries, Gemini, and Virgo. By applying Carnelian, one can promote good digestion. It encourages the formation of new blood cells. Bleeding gums are also helped by regular rinsing with Carnelian water. Drinking Carnelian water helps firm the skin by stimulating the circulation. Psychologically, Carnelian increases vitality and zest for life while enhancing stability and the courage to carry out our daily tasks."[19]

Book two: "Carnelian activates the first, second, and third chakras, bringing an influx of life force, sexual and creative energies, and assertive will. It is a powerful aid to those who wish to build confidence, courage, passion, and power within themselves.... Carnelian can aid in awakening the vital energies of the three lower chakras, increasing zest for living and the willingness to take the risks inherent in all strong actions."[20]

AN OCCULT HEARING OF THESE DESCRIPTIONS:

Carnelian is a being of spiritual force spread throughout the Cosmos, a being through whom spiritual beings come into interactions of force with other spirits. This being is force, relation, and purity all at once, keeping all spiritual activity in motion, a kind of spiritual circulation; it is a creative being of the unboundedness of Life, not life in the biological sense, but Life as the coming-into-being of action, movement, zest, heart, will, and spiritual power.

Aquamarine—Compendium Description:

Book one: "Aquamarine symbolizes peace. It encourages a gentle nature and personality in the wearer. Aquamarine is related to the throat chakra. For Aquarius it promotes friendship and love, while for Pisces it encourages awareness. Libras are warned against danger.... When placed on the third chakra it relaxes the solar plexus and digestive organs. It also protects against seasickness. A large Aquamarine placed in water overnight and used the following morning to wash the skin without rubbing too vigorously will alleviate allergies. Placed on swollen glands or worn round the neck, it will reduce the swelling. Chronic tonsillitis can be relived by wearing a necklace of Aquamarine.... Aquamarine has a beneficial effect on the thyroid gland and is helpful in the treatment of problems with the vocal cords and speech."[21]

Book Two: "These luminous blue gemstones are one of the wonders of the mineral kingdom. They are good for all types of calming and cooling, from hot flashes to anger, yet they also activate the throat chakra, assisting one in the clear communication of one's highest truth. They are stones of the Water element, bringing one in touch with the subconscious domains of spirit, and our deepest emotions. Their energy is as refreshing as a shower under a cool waterfall. Even though

Aquamarine calms, it does not put one to sleep. . . .
For women, Aquamarine lends the courage and clarity
to express one's inner knowing and it enhances intuitive abilities. . . . For men, Aquamarine helps dispel
emotional numbness and the difficulty men sometimes
experience in communicating their feelings."[22]

AN OCCULT HEARING OF THESE
DESCRIPTIONS:

Aquamarine is an angelic being of infinite peace and
calmness and an originator of spiritual friendship and
spiritual love in the universe. This being's qualities of
current are rhythmic, undulating, and fluid. It is a being
of higher service, oriented always to the cool and dis-
tant cosmic realms, and receiving constant refreshing
currents from those regions. It is a being of great and
vast interiority existing within the higher astral realms.

These revised descriptions, of course, still contain the
ego element. Nonetheless, the practice of going
through books about crystals, minerals, and stones
and holding the given descriptions inwardly until they
begin shifting from our desires and becoming more
like pictures of the qualities and characteristics that
belong to autonomous beings is a necessary reorient-
ing out of ego concerns and a first movement into
feeling the stone beings within our soul life. Rather

than the lion-like claws of our ego, eager to get hold of one of these stones in order to possess the described characteristics for ourselves, we instead begin to feel a reverence toward the spiritual realms and begin to turn toward their way of being.

Soul, in relation to something we sense, such as a stone, concerns the way in which an initial connection, made lovingly and carefully, continues to live on within us. If, for example, I look at a rose, notice its beauty and its fragrance, and sense the sweetness of it color—that is a sense experience. If I then turn away from the rose and move on to something else, that experience did not become a conscious soul experience. For it to be a soul experience, we have to be present to how the rose lives within us as we perceive it and how it continues to live on within us when we are no longer in its presence. Being present to the soul of the stone is, however, not something personal and private, although the way a stone is inwardly felt is very individual and is dependent on the degree of individual soul development. Soul, however, is never personal, having to do with the personality. Soul, while individually manifest, is at the same time a oneness with the soul of that with which we are in connection. Thus, to be present to the inner soul of a stone is to be at one with our soul and the soul of the stone—

and, in addition, one with the Soul of the World in one of Her intensities.

This step in working with stones—how the stone continues to live on within us when it is no longer present—is not mentioned in books of stones. It is something more than our reaction to the crystal or how we feel about it when we are with the stone. It takes a work of contemplation to be present with the stone in this way.

When we shut our eyes after a sensory experience with a stone, there is an "after-image"—an after-effect. This after-image is given as an inner, vivid, animated, activity: the stone in its action, not the stone as an inert thing that has magical properties. Being with a stone in this manner is the continuation of the sensing process spoken of earlier; it is what follows upon the careful focused/diffused gazing with reverence, with attention placed in the center of the heart for several minutes followed by closing one's eyes and waiting.

Sensing the stones as previously described takes us into an open awareness. This awareness cannot be filled with expectation; it is an attentive waiting, and all effort is oriented toward getting to the opening where proper waiting occurs—waiting for the unknown and unexpected without effort. The simultaneous sensing of a stone in a way that is both concentrated and openly aware suspends the usual chaining of the soul to the ego, making possible the dawning of another space of experience. In this new, open, interior space, flashes occur—instants in which everything stands still and the soul of the stone comes forth. We can practice being open to such moments, but the presence of such moments cannot be controlled; that is, they do not happen each time one contemplates a stone in this way. The fact that the soul of the stone does not reveal itself in the way objects in the world reliably do is not due to the absence of the soul of the crystal or mineral; it is more that we are not yet capable of living in the suspension of disbelief in a sustained way that allows the presence of the completely unknown to be present. Our mind intrudes, even without our knowing it is happening, and our mind cleverly figures out how to subvert the whole practice, again without our noticing the mind's continual manipulation for its own self-preservation in a position of power. Gradually, perhaps, once the tricks of the mind are recognized, the void opens more readily. But grace is the deciding factor, not us.

While the sensing practice spoken of earlier seems to rely heavily on vision, once we have entered the Silence and placed our attention in the center of the heart, usual sensing changes, gravitating more toward a synesthesia of the senses—that is, we are more present to the simultaneous activity of all sensing as occurring as one rather than the separation of the senses that we are used to. Thus, in the practice described below of working with the after-image, it is important to realize that the practice is not really visual, though vision is the metaphor carrying the synesthetic sensory experience. Touch, in particular, is central in the practice.

CONTEMPLATIVE PRACTICE II
Contemplation with the Soul of a Stone

If the first contemplative practice with stones is not carefully done, when you move on to this step the result will be fantasy and false imagination. All esoteric traditions recognize the difference between true and false imagination. Imagination is a higher form of sensing—the capacity of being present to the inner, soul dimension of sensing. It also, when combined with spirit activity, is the source of the inner activity of creating. The usual way we think of imagination, as "just imagining," is false. Imagination is the sensing of the inner soul-being of what we are inwardly united with.

A degree of inner forces of concentration is required to sense stones in the way described in the first contemplative practice. After carefully allowing your attention to notice and then to take in each quality of a stone, and gazing on the stone with focused and open awareness, close your eyes. Alertly, but with the same bodily openness as before, place the attention into the interior of your being, and wait. After a few moments you will begin to inwardly perceive the interior soul activity of the stone as a kind of after-image light of the stone. Again, if the first practice was not done carefully, with attention fully given to the stone in focused, diffuse sensing, this activity will not occur.

If the after-image does not appear, then, still with eyes closed, waiting, remember as vividly as possible each appearance of the stone as you took in what attracted you—the appearance when sensed through simultaneous focused and open awareness, not as you conceptually "sense" the stone in ordinary consciousness. You may see an after-image of the stone. It will be much like when you stare intently at a candle flame and then close your eyes and see an after-image of the flame of the candle. Such an after-image soon fades, then comes back, then fades again until it is no longer present. It "echoes" away. The after-image of the stone occurs in the same way. If the stone sits, for example, on a white piece of paper, when you close your eyes, you will see a black square. Within the square there is a form of light somewhat in the shape of the stone—though it may be of quite a different shape, because in gazing at the stone you also begin to sense the aura shining around the stone.

If this kind of visual after-image does not occur, do not immediately feel that something that was supposed to happen did not happen. The prime rule of any spiritual practice is to be present to and be able to describe what DOES happen, not what does not happen. The moment we get focused on the negative, we are outside of spiritual consciousness.

What is most important is to wait without expectation. Even more difficult, when something is noticed inwardly in the void following the echoing away of the after-image, allow its appearance to unfold without reacting in fear or expectation, bur rather remaining in a mood of equanimity, which is the equipoise between pleasure and displeasure. That is, this active waiting is within the place of the soul; soul lives in pleasure-displeasure, but as soon as you go toward one or the other, the ego will identify with one of these states. So, the waiting is waiting on the razor's edge.

You are in the interior world, so you should not wait for something to show up in the same way that you wait for something or someone to show up in the world of every-day life. Something "showing up" may occur in the form of a bodily sensation—just notice it, don't interpret it. Something "showing up" is always, in some manner or another, bodily felt. It often occurs as a feeling of "waving currents" that can almost be seen, but are much more felt than seen. When these kinds of qualities occur, dismiss any notion or inward feeling that this is just something "subjective." Once those kinds of notions are cleared, there begins to be a quite clear inner sense that what is happening is indeed the presence of the being of the stone. Still, even speaking this way tends to excite expectation, which has to be, at first, noticed and calmed. If nothing at all happens, that is just fine—this is the most helpful attitude to develop.

It takes time and great patience to be present to what occurs bodily—and for bodily sensitivity to develop. It is important to remember that here, in the interior world, you are still within body, and what appears inwardly is bodily, even if it is within the imagination of "seeing." You have entered into body-consciousness, which is different than the cognitive consciousness you usually have of the body in which the body is an object of cognition, sensing, or perception. In this practice, the inner being of the stone appears through body-consciousness, but there is no consciousness of the body per se.

This part of the Stone Path may take the longest to develop, or it may occur right away. If it does not occur right away, the most important response is continuing to try without becoming in any way frustrated.

What you inwardly see depends on the particularity of the stone. In the interior "luminous darkness." there will typically appear a lighting-up. You will inwardly know that you are "seeing" something and not making it up. If you begin to wonder whether you are making up what is present, push through that doubt and take what presents itself without judgment. The presence of doubt arises very subtly and quickly when it comes. I call it the "agnostic reflex," meaning there is an automatic doubter within each of us. Once it is there, it takes hold and the only thing to do is to stop and try again later. It is not necessary to consider what is going on inwardly and then question it, or try to examine it. This kind of doubt is much more sneaky that that. It is defeated by recognizing before-hand that it will indeed show up, and then dropping it the very second it comes to mind.

Once you have pushed through the "doubter," the whole inner experience of the after-image becomes more and more clearly the appearance of an autonomous presence, which you are within. It is not like looking at something in the sensory world, but it does have its own kind of objectivity.

If you are within fantasy rather than imagination, there is a strong presence of the ego with the appearance of the inner image, and you will find that you are at the center of the image. It is clearly not an act of perceiving, but an act of our desires being presented in image-like form.

Imagination is much more like sensing and perceiving. Something is simply present, though we are inwardly aware that this presence is also dependent on our participation, our creative presence with this presence. It is this way also with sensing or perceiving something in the outer world, but we are not aware of it. That is, we are not aware that what we sense is in part sensed because of the creative activity of our sensing-consciousness. In imagination, we are so close and infolded with the image that this relation is much more transparent.

While I am using the metaphor of "seeing" to refer to the appearance of the image, imagination is not visual. Imagination occurs in the realm of feeling, but it acts as if something is being seen. This manner of appearance indicates that feeling has become so strong that the presence of what we are in feeling connection with "appears." What will inwardly appear, besides an inner light, has a wide range of possibilities. In the interior of soul life, each stone appears differently. The most significant aspect of this appearance, though, is that it will be an activity. There will not be any kind of a static, inner thing. The image is also transparent, meaning that it is seen and "seen-through" at the same time, which is an indication of being within a subtle realm. There may be "lights," "colors," "movement," a pattern, or an intensification of the inner light and patterns followed by their fading or maybe disappearing and coming back. The imagination, because it is something that you may not have experienced in this way before, has no conceptual categories with which to recognize this image. Analogies will inwardly and spontaneously present themselves: "it is like a torrent of rushing water"; "it is like the appearance of a light that begins to move in a circular way, then becomes larger and larger" . . . the variations are endless.

Let the active felt-image take its course. After some practice, it becomes possible to tell when the imagination is at a kind of peak, or is waning and will not return. At first, when the waning begins to occur you may feel an inner anxiety because you don't want it to go away. After a while you will become comfortable with the image having its own way.

There will be, though, a crucial moment in the unfolding of the image, a moment when the movement to the next step has to take place or that next phase will not unfold. More of the nature of this moment is described in the next practice. It is often inwardly sufficient to be with the inner soul life of the stone and not go to the next phase.

It may take some time and practice to develop the capacity of being present with the soul-presence of the stone. The most crucial part of the practice is doing the first sensing practice very carefully. The stone cannot live within as a soul-presence unless it was carefully sensed in the first place. If it is not carefully sensed and is instead inwardly experienced, it will be a fantasy or a projection, not the actual soul-presence of the stone. We can tell it is the stone-as-soul-being because the living image within will have a strong autonomous quality to it. It is not exactly like looking at something in the world. The soul-presence is more diaphanous than that. And it is something that can only occur through our soul-being. Thus, the activity is something we are "seeing" while we are wholly within and a part of it at the same time. However, once this experience occurs, you will know forever the difference between inner seeing and engaging in fantasy. We have to put away, though, the list of attributes given in stone books, and even put away our re-visioning of the attributes as qualities of the angelic beings of the crystals and minerals. The purpose of that exercise was not to develop spiritual information, but rather to begin the practice and process of forming our beings into an adequate instrument. The reason attributes are not doled out by stones is because spiritual beings always belong to the Wholeness and thus help us by orienting us toward our Wholeness. The segmenting of our Wholeness into feelings of lacking something or needing something is in fact a symptom of the loss of Wholeness, not the symptom of a specific lack that can be filled by having that one separated thing. The spiritual beings of stones, however, present themselves *as if* promising specific qualities. The very nature of this internal perceiving is filled with anticipation. It is important to calmly enter into the quality of anticipation while releasing any mental notion that it has to result in something. Anticipation indicates the presence of something alive and active. It is really not anticipation at all; it is the coming-into-being of what is presenting itself.

Wholeness is not yet fulfilled through the soul-presence of the stone within our soul-being. But it is a necessary step that cannot be bypassed if we are engaged on this spiritual path. At the same time, it is important to avoid literalizing each of these steps. Different people have different ways of coming into fullness of connection with stones. As with any spiritual path, the path of stones is not about what stones can do for us; it is a way of body, soul, and world transformation. Unless we open our soul-beings completely to this way of working, false images intrude that always have the characteristic of trying to get something directly from crystals.

CHAPTER 4

The Spirit Worlds of Crystals and Minerals

It is helpful to develop a feeling for the spiritual-cosmic origins of crystals and minerals. We cannot just use the word "cosmic" without appearing vague and nondescript. With "cosmic," I speak first of returning the stones to the spiritually understood Zodiacal constellations of the Cosmos—and also to specific planets, stars and even galaxies. It is not in the least necessary, though, that we know where we are going when we enter into the spiritual world of a stone. I know that I don't know this information. Entering into the spiritual world of each stone, though, is certainly experienced as being within cosmic worlds and dimensions. I do not directly, cognitively know from which constellation, star, or planet the beings of the stones seem to originate. Some books on stones do correlate specific stones with specific constellations and planets, but do not indicate the source of this information.

Rudolf Steiner has written of the connection between certain stones and the twelve constellations of the

Zodiac. He has also given the relation between certain stones and certain stars. While there is a definite risk in indicating what those correspondences are, it is perhaps more helpful than harmful. It is not my intention to put forth the notion that, say, if you are a Capricorn you should work with the corresponding stone, which is Rose Quartz. And these correspondences have nothing to do with putting forth an astrology of stones. The purpose of indicating the correspondences Steiner gives, which he came to through his practiced clairvoyance, is solely and completely to provide a more refined sense of the spiritual origins and beings of stones, rather than just saying that we are partners in the return of spiritual presences of crystals and minerals to the Cosmos.

The constellations Steiner speaks of are also not quite the same as those stars patterns we see when we look at the night sky. He means the spiritual, creative angelic beings of those constellations. The hope is that this listing will inspire contemplation of the crystals mentioned in terms of these beings. There are certainly other crystals and minerals related to the constellations; it is not intended to be an exhaustive or exclusive list. These stones, though, would be central to work with in entering the living imagination of a new Earth.

Aries—Amethyst

Taurus—Garnet

Gemini—Jasper or Topaz

Cancer—Chrysolite

Leo—Beryl

Virgo—Peridot

Libra—Carnelian

Scorpio—Sardonyx

Sagittarius—Emerald

Capricorn—Chalcedony

Aquarius—Sapphire

Pisces—Jasper

This list is the same as the stones of the foundation of the New City given in the Book of Revelations:

Then came one of the seven angels . . . and said, "Come I will show you the bride, the wife of the Lamb." And in the spirit he carried me away to a great high Mountain and showed me the holy city of Jerusalem coming down out of heaven from God, having the glory of God, its radiance like an array of a Jewel, like a Jasper, clear as crystal. It had a great high wall with twelve gates and at the gates twelve angels and on the gates the names of the twelve tribes of the sons of Israel were inscribed; on the east three gates, on the north three gates, on the south three gates, and on the west three gates. And the wall of the city had twelve foundations and on them the twelve names of the twelve apostles of the land.... The wall was built of Jasper while the City was of pure gold as clear as glass. The foundations of the wall of the City was adorned with every jewel: in the first with Jasper, the second Sapphire, the third Chalcedony, the fourth Emerald, the fifth Sardonyx, the sixth Carnelian, the seventh Chrysolith, the eighth Beryl, the ninth Topaz, the tenth Chrysoprase, the eleventh Hyacinth, the twelfth Amethyst.

Crysolith is Peridot. Chrysoprase is the green form of Chalcedony, and Hyacinth is a form of Garnet, so the list corresponds perfectly. Through these correspondences we begin to get a feeling for the spiritual-cosmic world of stones. We also see that the spiritual path of stones works from the stones gradually outward, completely in and through the human being. We are used to working the other way—expecting, for example, that if I am a Libra, Carnelian will help me. The Stone Path would say that if I work inwardly with Carnelian, I am working with and for the enchanted Carnelian-beings. This, in turn, will initiate a circulation in which the beings of the stone, from their

"homes," inspire a particularity of our Wholeness—
and will also seed within our soul-spirit-being new
human capacities, capacities to be developed for the
future of humanity and of the Earth. These capacities
also help us each now, but in new, surprising, and
unknown ways. These new capacities are new structures of consciousness. With this path we work at the
very outer edge of what it is to be human. We begin
to discover that human capacities are not fixed, that
indeed we can, now, be transformative agents for a
new humanity that goes beyond anything we can fully
comprehend.

A contemplative way of uniting with the enchanted
crystal beings and freeing them into the spiritual Cosmos is based on the spiritual practices described by
The Mother, partner to Sri Aurobindo. It is the practice of identification. Here is her description of the
process of identification:

---

*"When I was in Paris," said Mother, "I used to go to
many places where all kinds of meetings were held by
people who were making all sorts of research, spiritual—so-called spiritual—and occult, etc. Once I
was invited to meet a lady who, I believe, was
Swedish—who had found a method of knowledge, precisely a method of learning. She explained that to us.*

We were three or four. Her French wasn't too good but, anyway, she was quite convinced. She said, 'Here, we take an object or draw a sign on a blackboard or we take a picture—it's immaterial, take whatever is easy for us!' She had a blackboard on which she drew a kind of semi-geometrical design. Well then, we sat in front of the design and concentrate our whole attention on it. We look and look and look, we become this design we are looking at. Nothing else exists in the world except the design, then, all of a sudden, we are through to the other side. And when we have passed to the other side we enter into a new consciousness, and we know. Oh, my! Is that what happened to Alice Through the Looking Glass?"[23]

Getting through to the other side—that is where we want to be able to go with a stone. We can get there by merging with the after-image of the stone. In this way, our spirit presence with the stone accompanies the spirit beings of the stone from the soul dimension into the other side, which is the spirit realm that is its origin and home. That is the spiritual intention of working with stones. It is a path requiring us to release conceptual sensing, enter into concentrated and open awareness, be present within the Silence and within the heart, be present to the soul presence of the stone inwardly, and then pour all attention into the soul-image. These "stages" are not to be taken literally, but they are very helpful for developing one's spiritual practice with stones. Sometimes, for example, being present to the soul-image of the stone spontaneously flows into entering the spirit-world of the stone.

Identification means that we pour all our forces of attention into the inner soul presence of the stone. We spiritually become the stone by lending all of our spirit forces to the stone. When we do so, it is as if we go through a membrane: the soul-image changes into a "landscape" of great beauty and each crystal or mineral is a particular landscape, a world filled with deep, unimaginable Silence and exquisite beauty. Whereas the after-image of a stone is often an active movement of patterns of light, the spirit-world of the stone is characterized more by its Silence and purity.

When we first inwardly perceive the spirit-world of a crystal, it may appear as something like the abandoned crystal world that was Superman's home. The Superman story seems in fact to be the concretized story of an angelic world that becomes devastated and of the descent of one of that world's beings to Earth, where it gives in service its powers, which are typically egotistically used by others to fulfill their needs. The angelic being can fly, even between worlds.

The only danger to this powerful being is that there is one stone that acts something like a radioactive stone, a stone that has completely fallen away from its cosmic origin, a stone connected entirely with those who want power for themselves, a stone that can kill this angelic presence. I'm convinced that the popular Superman imagination is a kind of intuition of the presence of angelic spiritual beings among us—though we would do better to look at stones than for a super-powerful human. When we enter the spiritual world of a mineral or crystal, that devastated, empty original world of the stones opens to incredible beauty and we inwardly experience the stone as having reentered a fullness of spirit-being. These worlds are not some-where far off. Linking stones with the Zodiac does not mean that the world of the stones is somewhere in space. The spiritual radiance of the stars of the Zodiac is all around us. Sometimes, when I have done the practice below, I have seen the light of the crystal fill the room. For example, the delicate pink of a Mor-ganite stone once filled the room. It conveyed, not in any language, but wordlessly, through the colors' pres-ence, the angelic qualities of Divine Love. I realized when that happened that our language is paltry, for the qualities of love experienced do not even come close to the actual presence of the living action of the crystal force.

The strongest experience of this stage of the Stone Path is that of suddenly finding ourselves on the other side of ourselves. It's difficult to describe. When we have merged with the stone we lose the usual sense of ourselves, but do not become in any way unconscious in doing so. We are not in trance or in any dream-like state. There is in fact a remarkable clarity to our consciousness, but it is a consciousness completely merged with the stone. We are still very individual, but there is the complete absence of any self-consciousness. In our usual state of ego consciousness, there is a sense that we are always looking at ourselves. In fact, we are. All of the things of this world, and others, are continually mirroring to us who we are. But only from the outside. Working with the mineral world changes that point of view and we become all at once the consciousness of the stone, the stone beings, and the content of the stones' world.

Here is a practice for entering into the spirit-presence of a stone and moving from the soul dimension into the spirit dimension of the stone, into its world.

CONTEMPLATIVE PRACTICE III
Entering the Spirit World of Stones

This practice must be preceded by the two former practices. It is not effective if done alone. While it may take some time to do the three practices all together, after you become accustomed to them, the time lessens considerably, not only because you have become practiced and more at ease, but, more significantly, because you have structurally changed—you have released the need to live so much from the domain of habits, and now inhabit more of your spirit nature.

The stone must be perceived, carefully and lovingly, in the Silence, through the heart, in concentrated and open awareness. Following this perceiving, upon closing your eyes, there must be an after-effect of the empathetic perceiving—a strongly felt image that you are able to describe. This image (not visual, but visual-like) will be like the after-image that occurs when staring at a candle flame and then closing the eyes.

In order for there to be this kind of inner soul-presence of the stone, it is necessary that the soul be "saturated" with the physical characteristics of the stone. When there is this after-effect, it will be active rather than a static "picture." It will also be present, fade, and then come back several times. When the after-effect is present, at a point of your choosing, not mentally, but from heart-feeling, then very actively pour all of your forces of attention into that after-effect. This concentration of forces is felt within the body—almost as a physical straining. It is a very active moment of the practice. You are going into the after-image, identifying with it, and merging with it. As you do so, you will notice that your eyelids begin to flutter—it is like the movement of the eyelids that can be seen when one observes another person dreaming, except you are very awake and alert while your attention is strongly focused but at the same time very open.

If you feel even an inclination for the eyelids to flutter, then go into that fluttering and exaggerate it a little by putting will forces there. You will feel as if you are going through a "membrane," through the image, and out the other side. The eyelid flutter may become very strong. When you are on the "other side," relax the eyelids and notice what begins to form: you will "see" the world of the crystal—which may be geometric forms, forms like galaxies, complicated and beautifully colored "land-scapes," or other kinds of forms. The prevailing quality is the presence of Silence beyond Silence.

The intention of this identification process lies beyond inwardly seeing these quite amazing crystal worlds. By far, the most important aspect of this part of the stone practice follows after this new after-image recedes, echoes away, and there is nothing present other than deepest Silence. It is within this Silence that the stone as spirit-being is responding. Exactly at the point at which the "visual" or "feeling" effect ceases, practice being completely open, alert, and in full open-awareness within the void. We seek to sustain our presence in this void in order to welcome all things, without expectations. What occurs within this void is vividly felt; but it is wordless.

It is helpful to take up some sort of artistic practice as integral to this stage of the Stone Path. Artistic activity serves as a mirroring of the wordless, but nonetheless incredibly full, feeling experienced in the void. Drawing, painting, sculpting (or photography, as shown by the cover picture of this book), or rhythmic words such as poems or mantras not only express the experience but themselves become meditative tools for remaining close to the felt experiences within the void. Even more significant, however, you will begin to notice experiences in life that are clearly reflections of the felt voids—usually experiences of synchronicity, but also of waking with creative thoughts, spiritual thoughts that can be put into action. It is crucial to develop some mode of reflecting the experience of the spiritual worlds of the stones. Such a practice, which may be as simple as keeping a journal but allowing images to flow rather than "reporting" what happened, assures that the realms of fantasy and illusion do not enter. Without this essential step of becoming a researcher on the path taken, old and unconscious desires will subtly take over.

While within the mineral or crystal world, you may with soul and feeling inwardly, gesturally, speak with that crystal world. When we are within the depth of the spiritual worlds like this, words become forces; words are no longer indicators of concepts, but are action, action of the same type as that of the spiritual worlds you are within. When you inwardly gesture a word you may, for example, let your mouth silently say the word or words. Speak very slowly, saying the next word only when you have felt the resonance of the word-as-power reverberate within your bodily being.

Realize, however, that the response from the spirit world of minerals and crystals will always be in the form of a spiritual capacity rather than a literal response. Notice during the next three days following the stone meditation what you inwardly feel, the general tone or mood, and also how the world appears, what happens. As you work with stones in this way, there will be the inner development of a sense of thinking, feeling, and doing from an entirely different place than previously. You will feel an inner capacity to act more out of spiritual freedom, and to be with others and the world with a felt closeness to the spiritual worlds.

Once we establish familiarity with the three contemplative practices with crystals and minerals—and for a while we are able to put aside what we may want or need that the spiritual resonances of the mineral world might provide—we can revisit the descriptions from favorite books on stones, meditatively reading the indications of what stones provide at the physical, soul, and spiritual level. We will not feel the same way about these lists as we did before taking these few steps on the Stone Path. The characteristics of stones in the various lists in books can now be seen as a grammar of stones; that is, the "speech" of the stones themselves can now be heard in the descriptions given by the books. This inner change in our capacity to feel what is happening in working with crystals and minerals concerns the nature of intuition, which has been entered into through the practices.

Intuition is the way of becoming one with a stone, the way of entering into its reality, its world, its consciousness. We no longer stand outside of it and observe it with our ego-consciousnesses; we also pass through the inner, soul process of witnessing the spiritual being of the stone through our soul-being. Our witnessing of an image and being filled with its reality belong to the processes of imagination and inspiration. In both of these processes, there is the felt presence of the inner witnessing. The witnessing is that inner quality of being united with the life of the stone while still retaining an inner sense of a special kind of observation—one in which we inwardly experience something of the stone's interior being resonating, while we are still also aware of ourselves as interior "observers," but not detached.

Witnessing is something entirely different than the kind of spectator-like looking that characterizes ego consciousness. We feel within and part of what we witness at the soul level. What is actually occurring, however, is that the inner spirit-being of the stone has gifted us, has entered into our soul-beings and is one with them. When we actively place the whole of our attention into the soul-presence of the stone, there is a reversal of the reversal. The first reversal is to go from being a spectator to allowing the stone-being into our souls—an essential act of love for a spiritual being. The second reversal is to then engage in a purely spiritual act of love by "becoming" the being of the stone. This second reversal thus means experiencing currents of selfless love pouring from us rather than always being on the lookout for love we might be receiving.

It is important to have an understanding of this process, though far more important to engage in it. With intuition, we become the stone without losing any sense of ourselves in the process.

When the intuitive contemplation is completed and there is a return to more usual consciousness, there is the felt-sense of the stone's spirit-being. The whole process, from the first physical perceiving to the full intuitive moment, often takes place very, very quickly. Those who have the gift of this kind of engagement have usually come to it without tracking their own process. All that I have presented here is simply a tracking of that process in order to experience it more slowly and more vividly within. The moment of intuition shifting back into more usual consciousness typically converts or translates the intuitive sense of the stone's inner spirit-life back into usual consciousness. The result of that perhaps too-quick transition to usual consciousness is that the spirit-being consciousness of the stone is translated into wholly human terms.

For example, there are a host of stones that are said to "give" us a feeling of and even the capacity for courage. Robert Simmons lists some of these stones in his *Book of Stones:*

Albite, Golden Apatite, Clear Apophyllite, Bixbite, Black Phantom Quartz, Bloodstone, Carnelian, Cuprite, Emerald, Hematite, Heulandite, Red Jade, Marcasite, Snowflake Obsidian, Peridot, Ruby, Sphalerite, Sugilite, Golden Tourmaline, Dravite, Vesuvianite.

Quite a list. Let's take one, Albite, and look at the "grammar" of the stone as spoken by Simmons:

Albite helps one to view the chaotic-seeming kaleidoscope of life events through the ordering activities of a strong mental body. It stimulates the part of the mind which creates categories, hierarchies and structures, making it easier for one to prioritize one's choices and sustain projects through to completion. . . . Albite is a stone of decisive action, enhanced confidence, courage, and willingness to enter the unknown.[24]

This sense of the stone's qualities comes from intuition. The speaking of that intuition tends to take the form of known concepts that are going to be understood by the reader in terms of ordinary consciousness.

When some version of the practices described in this writing is taken up, the spiritual nature of the descriptions given usually begins to light up in a new way. First of all, the spiritual courage of the designated stones in our example belongs to the elemental and creative spiritual beings of the stones. The spirit-beings of the stones take us into *their spiritual performance of the quality* when we enter into stone intuition, or stone-consciousness. The stone is not some thing that gives the quality of courage. The stone *is* an action of *spiritual courage.* And *spiritual courage* is something different than what we know as "courage." If the stones are resonances of spirit activity, then we have to look at what enters us from them as *spiritual capacities*—that is, capacities of an individual in the process of developing now as a spiritual human being. As said earlier, this is a different quality of being than a human being who does spiritual things; it is our entrance into acting as spiritual beings of the Earth. Spiritual courage differs from the ability, for example, to perform acts of heroism. It differs from the ability to perform difficult deeds, face extremely difficult life circumstances, or to perform an act completely for the sake of someone else; it also has little to do with having power.

"Practical spiritual action" is a good synonym for the kind of spiritual courage inspired by the stones listed above. Under such an inspiration, a person's whole life and being becomes an inner dedication toward moving always forward, with perseverance—toward union with the spirit. This perseverance completely lacks the aim of gaining any material advantage. It is, however, not an "escapist" virtue either—it is not perseverance toward a spiritual world that lies somewhere else. It is perseverance in seeing, feeling, sensing, and acting in accordance with the spiritual dimensions of individual life and the life of the world. Perseverance occurs in the absence of any surrounding support, and without the sense of gaining anything for oneself in the strictly material sense.

When worked with in the great circulation that begins with our working with the spiritual beings of the stones to free them from enchantment, these stones transform bodily will into spiritual act. Spiritual courage concerns the alignment of our actions with the higher consciousness of our spirit individuality. Spiritual courage is the ability to move in soul both vertically and horizontally at the same time, to be in a relation of fullness with the world and the spiritual worlds simultaneously. The stones do not "give" us spiritual abilities, but rather the potential for them: the awakening of a consciousness that unfolds into these abilities through an alchemical transformation of body and soul. Working with the Stone Path is like learning a whole new life, an entirely new level of being. If we do not inwardly develop from an egotistic place of utilizing stones to give us certain abilities to becoming partners with spirit-beings interested in the great future unfolding of a new Humanity and a new Earth, working with stones will recede into a spiritual egotism.

The qualities of stones given in the books can now be felt in a new way. Every stone, worked with as a spiritual path, transforms us in body, soul, and spirit. Some stones do so more intensively at the bodily level, some at the soul level, and some at the spirit level of our beings.

CHAPTER 5

Three Examples of Spiritual Practice with Stones

The three examples below are intended to show what working with stones as spiritual practice is like. What follows cannot in any way be compared with a compendium of stones. Stone compendia are typically filled with big claims, easily leading to inflation. These examples are nothing more than three small attempts to speak something of the processes that have been described. The examples also indicate how difficult it is to take up a spiritual stance, stay within it without straying in and out of old consciousness, and refrain from making claims that go beyond what is actually experienced. These examples are also not intended to be prescriptive, that is, they are not descriptions of what ought to happen with these stones when working with them in the ways pictured thus far. Working with stones as spiritual practice builds the capacity of individuality, the capacity of the spiritual "I," the capacity to be conscious in an embodied way in the higher self. Those who work meditatively with stones in this manner will not experience the same things at all. Thus, a compendium simply would not work. However, because a capacity is being developed, those who engage these practices can track and describe exactly what happens and convey that knowledge to others; others, who work in a similar manner with stones are immediately able not only to understand the experiences of others, but to see how they are variations of their own experiences.

Rosophia

Rosophia is a stone recently discovered as having metaphysical importance by Robert Simmons. In his book *Stones of the New Consciousness* he tells a long story of his discovery of this stone and describes meditative interactions with this stone. The actual description can be summarized as a mixture of reddish Feldspar, clear or white Quartz, and black Biotite. Much more is given in Simmons's book concerning the discovery of this stone and its felt qualities.

As I describe working meditatively with this stone by way of the stages and practices described throughout this writing, a caution is necessary. Each individual will experience this process somewhat differently. The particular content will be different for each individual, and the experience will change depending on what degree of inner soul development continues to occur for a person working with the stone. Nonetheless, it is possible to describe the experiences in such a manner that the *flow* and *form* of experiences can be followed by anyone making the effort. And if this flow and form is followed, while the content of the experiences will differ for different people, their inner essences will coincide. In addition, when the practices given in this writing are repeated over and over with the same stone, more qualities unfold because the spirit beings of the stone reveal themselves in accordance with where we are within our own soul livs. As that grows and changes, more and varied spiritual qualities of the stone emerge.

The stone I work with is a polished sphere. I start by stilling the mind, entering into the Silence, and placing my attention at the center of my heart. I notice the way in which, with this polished Rosophia sphere, there is a overlapping blending of three different colorings—red, white, and black—a kind of patterning, almost like a quilting. This patterning is felt inwardly too—it is not just an outer configuration. The inward feeling in the place of the heart is one of intense intimacy, a bringing together, in feeling, of three realms of intimacy—one deep and dark, one cosmic, and one heart-felt. These feeling qualities do not exist side by side, but interpenetrate one another. The feeling is not given in this "analytic" way; there is only the feeling of an intimacy interweaving with longing, interweaving with joy. Each of these qualities of the experience as described here are "borrowed" from experiences we have all had and with which we are familiar. The interweaving of them is something different and can only be deeply felt; there are no concepts to reveal what the experience is like, and at this stage in the process there are only inklings of it.

I look lovingly at a patch of the light, almost pinkish red, and can see into the transparent overlapping white, pulling the attention toward the center of the stone, which now can be felt as a drawing of feelings from the center of the heart to the stone's center. I then close my eyes and feel the presence of that color inwardly. This little moment is of immense significance for the stone. It is the moment of my taking it into the heart by letting what I sense and feel permeate my being; it is the initial moment of becoming one with the stone. I don't dwell long with that inner color—I just notice the felt quality of its intimacy. I then open my eyes and other colors and forms within the stone get my attention. Each time a quality of the stone draws my attention to it, I look, then close my eyes, and let the color/form of what I was seeing now live within me simultaneously as memory, image, and feeling. I work

with the stone in this manner in sittings of twenty minutes or so for several days; the stone changes from being
an external object of some interest to the sense of a
feeling of how precious it is; it is as if we have become
acquainted with each other. It is the interior space that
now exists between us that feels significant. I can leave
this space and return to seeing the stone as an outer
object, but when I do so all feelings with it diminish.

Following this befriending of the stone, I start the
meditation again, gazing at the stone again but as if
for the first time. This time, after sensing the stone for
a good while, I close my eyes and let the ardor within
my heart be with the inner-felt qualities of the stone.
Intense attention. Then, inwardly, emerald green flowing forms of light accompanied with patches of black
appear. The flowing form of the color reminds me of
the aurora borealis, but that is an imposed concept,
so I drop it and just stay connected with the unfolding of the light. The colors appear quite suddenly and
I feel a bit of a shock. It is necessary in this kind of
contemplation to get to the point of just noticing these
kinds of occurrences without reacting to the force of
them, as any reaction will pull us out of what is happening. It is as if there has been an inner movement—
from a kind of inner repetition of the sensory
experiences of the stone, which is something like "lift-

ing" the color away from the hardness of the stone to an inner sensing and feeling of the color becoming its own life: it—the stone—begins to appear on its own terms as having animated qualities. I notice the green, flowing forms that are somewhat incandescent and I now realize that the endlessly deep patches of black are also "light." The black does not appear as though it were a wall of black; it has depth and its own kind of clarity, which pulls me deeply down into a similar place of dark, luminous clarity within myself.

As these colors appear, I then will my full attention into the colors—particularly the emerald green incandescence. It is as if I pick up my attention with my hand and usher it closer and closer to the colors until it begins to merge into the flow of colors. Attention has the amazing quality of being able to do things in relation to itself without splitting off from itself. The colors are moving and also fading and coming back, so there has to be a moment of decision without thinking—an immediate moving of attention fully into a color when it seems it is at its most intense.

When attention is focused on the colors, it is also possible to notice that I am "witnessing" what is occurring. This witnessing is the act of attention itself, so it is attention to attention, and it is possible to pour that attention fully into the color. When I do so, the green/black disappears. Then at first there is a muted gold radiance that is lighted from within itself and has no boundaries, but it does have what feels like infinite depth. I also feel an inward lightness of feeling, a kind of buoyancy, and in that buoyancy my heart knows that the beings of the stone are now freed and *are* this golden light. It is not as if I am inwardly just "looking at" this golden light. There is nothing other than the golden light, and it is experienced, not as "within" me, but as completely surrounding me and I am within it as pure consciousness. I am not within it as a bodied form, but I am not "out of body" either. The "I" here does consist of a felt-sense of an invisible form, but it does not have the solidity of my body as I usually experience it. It is itself like a condensation at the center of this golden light.

I wait. Then, I feel, right in the center of the heart, the visitation of a very strong current of warmth and love, but it is not like any feeling of warmth and love experienced before; it is much freer, as there is no felt quality of wanting this feeling or being inwardly concerned that it will go away. The feeling is clearly and intrinsically given as the response of the spiritual stone beings, as it feels as if someone has placed deep and cosmic love in the center of my being. It is like an initiation into a new form or kind of love.

I remain with this feeling within the heart for a while, then inwardly thank the stone beings for their presence. I remain still within an inner void that is filled with the quality of the new form of love: love that is oriented toward a unity of Earth and human beings. But it is not as general as this sounds; it is a very specific and particular love-as-force. It is love freed from sensuality. After a time, I open my eyes. The whole process lasted probably twenty minutes or less.

Once this kind of contemplation with a stone occurs, the stone now lives within and it is quite easy to return to the inner beings of the stone at any time. With this stone, for example, what seems to come in the Great Circulation is the root of a capacity for a new kind of love. It is like being able, in one moment, to love the heart, soul, and spirit of another person, to experience that same kind of intimate love with everything around me, and to experience the Earth intimately and closely.

I notice that I am able to be within this capacity for about three days, but only when I consciously and inwardly return to the feeling of the stone. The moment I do, the whole experience is present and I feel the whole of my being transfigured into a form that accommodates this love as integral to my being. After that time, the capacity fades from its intensity, but the new quality of love is something permanent that can be returned to any time. It is extremely interesting that the spiritual capacities engendered in working with stones do not become a habit. These new human possibilities are present only when we are aware of them.

Aragonite

Robert Simmons describes the physical appearance of Aragonite as: "a calcium carbonate mineral with a hardness of 3.5 to 4. It occurs in various colors, including white, gray, reddish, yellow-green, and blue. Aragonite's crystal system is orthorhombic, and it can be found in prismatic crystals, concretions, stalactitic masses, or other forms...."[25] I worked with an Aragonite from Spain. It is prismatic, white and purple, with multiple interlocking crystals that are striated and shiny.

The contemplative way of being with the sprit-beings of the crystals does not always "work." It is very important to remember the purity of the mineral world. If we feel anything other than the purest of love for stones, with the strongest ardor of the heart, I suspect that they remain hidden from the contemplations.

I have had several different experiences with the Aragonite. The first time a clear engagement with the world of the crystal occurred, but there was no felt sense of the circulation back from the stone beings; that is, there was not some kind of response from the beings of this world within the void of Silence at the end of the contemplation. A second time, nothing much happened, but I recognized that I had begun to make the process into a kind of formula to be gone through to get to where I anticipated wanting to be. Like any meditative practice, each time one does the practice it has to be done new and fresh and what previously happened cannot be relied on without entering into a spectator perspective.

The third time was somewhat different. Upon entering into the Silence and then placing attention in the center of the heart, there was a felt sense of ardor for the crystal beings. I could feel the resonance of the stone, which is very, very high and fine, and I could not quite adjust my body's resonance to be perfectly in tune with the stone's resonance. But it felt close. I suspect that the first two times, when the contemplation did not work so well, were due to the high vibrational qualities of the stone that I did not initially recognize. The result of my missing that quality was that nothing could occur, as the intensity of vibration was numbing the bodily receptivity. Once I worked at adjusting my body resonance to the stone's resonance, the process of perceptually allowing what shined in the physical presence of the stone to be taken into the heart went well. I felt the strong light reflections, the shining glitter of the stone's surface, move from outward sensing to an inward presence of the stone's surface, which I perceive as a strong mirroring that invites the gaze into the stone while at the same time pushing the gaze away.

Another visual aspect of the stone consists of the vertical form of the crystal, and the multiple "stacking" of the crystal, as if it had been built from the center outward in a series of tightly connected crystal forms. The deep purple spots of color here and there in the stone were also taken into the heart, one by one.

While I held all these qualities inwardly, waiting, a vertical, ice-like, narrow form, like a frozen waterfall appeared. As I stayed with that presence, it felt as if this white-silver crystallized form was lit from within. I poured all of my attention and will forces into this form, trying to "go into it." It felt like going through a membrane; the eyes fluttered, a bit like it must be when one is dreaming at night. When that fluttering occurs, which it does each time I do a contemplation with a stone, I exaggerate it a bit by going even further into the body and putting my will forces into the fluttering. Then, merging with the after-image and going through the membrane occurs.

There is a sudden calmness. The fluttering stops and there is the presence of golden light. With this crystal, there was a "center" to the golden light, a center that seemed to be moving in a counter-clockwise direction, looking somewhat like a galaxy or like a radiating sun—somewhere between the two. At this moment, there was the felt sense of the stone being's freedom. It is a quality that is simply present: it comes unannounced, and is unmistakable. Then, it feels as if nothing is happening, and I have to remind myself to be still and just wait.

After a few moments, a streak of silvery light was present. It was not static, but rather was an intense movement. Whereas previously the light had a slight silvery tinge to it, this was far more silvery, and it bore the quality of joy within it. I felt joy, but it was not a feeling originating in me but rather a visitation from the light. There was also the inherent feeling of "wealth." The feeling is most difficult to describe: it is firm, solid, strong, and a feeling and not a thought. It did bring the thought of monetary wealth—of silver as wealth, but that was clearly an inner association and it was very clear that this was not the feeling of "wealth." It was not something, for example, that signified wealth, but its immediate presence. It is something more akin to strength and perhaps to courage.

The inner quality is one that is like a strong wealth of courage-for-life.

These felt-qualities of response from the spiritual worlds of the stones are difficult to describe because they are entirely new and completely unfamiliar. There are no available words or concepts for the felt qualities. In addition, the experience itself occurs in the deepest Silence and is wholly in the realm of feeling. It is quite likely that these "return-responses" from the beings of the stones are a seeding of the new human being— something to be fully developed in the far future and not likely to occur in this lifetime. The qualities are felt as visitations; they are very strong and remain after the contemplation is completed. They can quite easily be reentered just by recalling not the qualities themselves, but the inner image of the stone's felt qualities as they appeared in the contemplation.

After the contemplation was completed, strong inner after-images continued to appear. The images were of a cascading, purple-gray, cloud-like formation, though of firmer substance than clouds. These forms appeared in a strong vertical direction and bore a strong feeling quality—a quality of inner strength, inner illumination and beauty.

Golden Azeztulite

This way of contemplation with stones requires a great deal of inner effort. One of the interesting questions is, why it does not work each time? I have explored this question some with this stone, Golden Azeztulite, because at first there was virtually no after-image occurrence. When I looked inwardly to what was going on, I discovered that I had an intellectual interest in the stone but had not really made a heart connection with it. When this happens, it is not to be judged—as if one did not "do it right"; rather, I took this first try as an instance of getting acquainted with the crystal. Indeed, the next day inner feeling toward the stone occurred quite frequently. In fact, it occurred so much and so strongly that the following evening when I again approached working with the crystal, there was an inner confidence that we would make connection. This confidence did not come from me, but appeared quite suddenly, probably due to my making a caring gesture toward the stone. Even before doing a preliminary contemplative alignment and placing attention in the center of the heart, there were very strong currents coming from the stone that I could feel as I held it—currents that were not felt the night before. Inner images of light began appearing before I began any actual work with the crystal.

Then, the contemplation occurred. The outer surface of the small crystal is so interesting. One face of the crystal is slightly bent inward, making a bow, a slight convex form. And the face has a number of slight edges; that is, it is not a completely smooth face. As I look at this face through the place of the heart, I feel drawn into it, so I close my eyes and take that aspect of the crystal in.

At the top of this face, on the right edge, there is a distinct form of a small triangle. I am familiar with some Quartz having these triangles, which are said to be "record-keepers," holding memories of past ages. I wonder if that is what this form is, though it is much stronger, much deeper than any such form I have seen before. After observing this triangle with heart-awareness, I close my eyes and let the image repeat, now in an inner way.

In a few moments, there is a feeling of inner pressure. When I notice this pressure, through an inner act of will I exaggerate the felt pressure and my eyes start to flutter. Again through an act of will, I exaggerate this feeling. Then, there is an inner burst of extremely strong white light; it is a light, though, that is illuminated from within and thus carries the sense of it being living light. The light takes the form of a central ball of intense white light, and from this ball there are innumerable filaments of light spraying out and around. The filaments of light appear crystalline-like, while at the same time they are pure light. It is almost inwardly blinding. I then let the will forces that I am applying relax, but the fluttering of the eyes continues, and this lets me know that a process is going on and that it is not yet completed. So I let it go on—more of the light. Then I relax again, and there is the presence of a calm, yellow light that I am within.

The strongest feeling with this crystal is that what is being released is the crystalline form that has been given/gifted to the human being. That is, this Azeztulite has brought the human being an inner light, and now this is being released. As I wait in the Silence, there is then the extremely strong feeling within the body of being everywhere a crystal. And there is an inner after-image occurring within the void of Silence, an image that is also a completely bodily experience and a vision of an utterly, completely transparent crystal that has only the barest outlines at the edges. The crystal, fully embodied, rotates counter-clockwise. The interiority of the crystal is pure invisibility. The response from the crystal beings is one of granting a sense that the true physical body is an invisible body. The feeling of the vision is that this is what the human being is intended to become, that is, pure transparency.

This crystal does not give us the gift of the Light Body. The inward seeing of the clear crystal form in itself is very enigmatic. The image has to be felt and inwardly experienced and the crystal has to be worked with on an ongoing basis. Only then will something as yet unknown begin to gradually unfold that slowly reveals what these crystal beings are offering.

The spiritual path of stones, in its unique way of freeing the enchanted beings of crystals and minerals, holds the sense that minerals and crystals are "worlds" that have become self-enclosed. But the surplus of the spiritual forces, in conjunction with the elemental beings, still affects us and provides the way into close connection with stones in order to be spiritual partners in returning them to their source. I don't imagine the stones as being exiled; the crystal beings chose this sacrifice of forming the solidity of Earth while imbuing Earth with spiritual forces. Through our effort of helping their return, a further cycle of creating of Earth and Human Beings can then occur. I know of no other spiritual path where the whole purpose of spiritual practice is for something other than individual transformation. Such transformation happens on this path, too, but it is secondary, an added bonus, so to speak. The result of this work is a healing that ranges from a healing of the Earth to the bringing of individuals into their Wholeness. The ultimate purpose of the work is waking to the Light Body—individually and of the Earth, though the full unfolding of the process may take ages.

Awakening through the mineral world does not suddenly come about. Experiences will occur rather readily working with minerals and crystals. These experiences reflect what is happening with the spiritual beings of the mineral worlds. How *we* change unfolds more slowly and the immediate experiences with the stones should not be taken to be experiences of our transformation. Rather, it becomes an ongoing work, not so different than the spiritual contribution each of us is making through the ordinary work that we do in the world. We do the work daily, and only very gradually see the inner transformation that has been wrought. The dangers of inflation are always present. Because some of the experiences with stones can be very strong and powerful, it may seem that the work is to have such experiences. Seeking spiritual experiences would result in inflation. The transformations of our being are more subtle and of more lasting value than what we experience along the way. The humbleness of this path will be very apparent when we enter the next phase.

Needed: a community of researchers into the Stone Path. Because so much work with stones is from a New Age perspective, the development of the Stone Path constitutes a large effort. The differences between the Stone Path and other approaches is sometimes subtle, and this work could easily be swallowed up into approaches oriented toward deriving gifts from crystals rather than developing capacities. Beginnings are always vulnerable. Further research involves refining the practices, working with more stones, and developing capacities for experiencing stones in relation with many different planets, stars, and constellations. The most significant aspect of further research concerns how this path is a path of practical spirituality. We are completely used to—addicted to—knowing in advance what is going to happen as a result of what we do; a scientific mentality has invaded and taken over consciousness. We do not know how to be within acausal actions and do not know how to allow the force of an inner connection with spiritual beings to unfold in life, nor do we know how to observe and track this kind of unfolding. Working with stones in the ways suggested here can be of great help in the development of practical, social, and Earth-oriented mystical experience.

The work of this book and the work projected is now available online. The website for the Stone Path is www.thecrystalspirits.com. Ongoing work with minerals and crystals is presented on the site as well as ways in which we can be of help to others in developing practices with stones.

Notes

1. Robert Simmons, *Stones of the New Consciousness: Healing, Awakening, and Co-creating with Crystals, Minerals, and Gems* (Berkeley: North Atlantic Books, 2009).

2. See Dennis Klocek, *Seeking Spirit Vision* (Sacramento, CA: Rudolf Steiner College Press, 1998), 255–264.

3. Rudolf Steiner, *The Mission of the Archangel Michael* (Great Barrington: Anthroposophic Press, 1961), 94.

4. Cited in Stephen Mitchell, *The Enlightened Heart* (New York: Harper & Row, 1989), 155.

5. Robert Sardello, *Silence: The Mystery of Wholeness* (Berkeley: North Atlantic Books/ Goldenstone Press, 2008).

6. Satprem, *Sri Aurobindo or the Adventure of Consciousness* (New York: Harper and Row, 1968).

7. Rudolf Steiner, *True and False Paths of Spiritual Investigation* (New York: Anthroposophic Press, 1985), 61.

8. Rudolf Steiner, *Occult Reading and Occult Hearing* (London: Rudolf Steiner Press, 1975), 57.

9. Robert Simmons, *The Book of Stones: Who They Are and What They Teach* (Berkeley: North Atlantic Books/Heaven and Earth Publishing, 2007).

10. For the best available description of the qualities of stones, such as transparency and color and form, see

Siegfried Heinz-Jurgen Ahlborn, *Sterne, Mensh, und Edelsteine* (Borchen: Verlag Ch. Mollmann, 1999).

11. Rudolf Steiner, *True and False Paths of Spiritual Investigation* (New York: Anthroposophic Press, 1985), 62.

12. Konrad von Megenberg, Franz Pfeiffer, ed, *Das Buch der Nature: Die erste Naturgeschichte in deutscher Sprache* (Hildesheim: G. Olms, 1962, 1971).

13. Rudolf Steiner, *Ursrungsimpulse der Geisteswissenschaft. Chrislike Esoterik Im Lichte neuer Geist-Erkenntnis (Christian Esotericism in the Light of new Spirit Knowledge)* (Dornach: Rudolf Steiner Verlag. Haus Duldeck, 1909).

14. Damigeron, Patricia P. Tahil, trans., *The Virtues of Stones* (Seattle: Ars Obscura Press, 1989), 29.

15. Robert Simmons, *The Book of Stones: Who They Are and What They Teach* (Berkeley: North Atlantic Books/Heaven and Earth Publishing, 2007), 351.

16. Ibid., 270

17. Rudolf Steiner, *From Jesus to Christ* (London, Rudolf Steiner Press, 2005).

18. Ibid., 113.

19. Flora Peschek-Bohmer and Gisela Schreiber, *Healing Crystals and Gemstones: From Amethyst to Zircon* (Old Saybrook, CT: Konecky and Konecky, 2003), 109.

20. Robert Simmons, *The Book of Stones: Who They Are and What They Teach* (Berkeley: North Atlantic Books/Heaven and Earth Publishing, 2007), 92.

21. Flora Peschek-Bohmer and Gisela Schreiber, *Healing Crystals and Gemstones: From Amethyst to Zircon* (Old Saybrook, CT: Konecky and Konecky, 2003), 114.

22. Robert Simmons, *The Book of Stones: Who They Are and What They Teach* (Berkeley: North Atlantic Books/Heaven and Earth Publishing, 2007), 50.

23. Sujata Nahar, *Mirra the Occultis, Volume Three* (Paris: Institute of Evolutionary Research, 1999), 84.

24. Robert Simmons, *The Book of Stones: Who They Are and What They Teach* (Berkeley: North Atlantic Books/Heaven and Earth Publishing, 2007), 18.

25. Robert Simmons, *Stones of the New Consciousness* (Berkeley: North Atlantic Books/Heaven and Earth Publishing, 2009), 134.

ABOUT
GOLDENSTONE PRESS

Goldenstone Press seeks to make original spiritual thought available as a force of individual, cultural, and world revitalization. The press is an integral dimension of the work of the School of Spiritual Psychology. The mission of the School includes restoring the book as a way of inner transformation and awakening to spirit. We recognize that secondary thought and the reduction of books to sources of information and entertainment as the dominant meaning of reading places in jeopardy the unique character of writing as a vessel of the human spirit. We feel that the continuing emphasis of such a narrowing of what books are intended to be needs to be balanced by writing, editing, and publishing that emphasizes the act of reading as entering into a magical, even miraculous spiritual realm that stimulates the imagination and makes possible discerning reality from illusion in the world. The editorial board of Goldenstone Press is committed to fostering authors with the capacity of creative spiritual imagination who write in forms that bring readers into deep engagement with an inner transformative process rather than being spectators to someone's speculations. A complete catalog of all our books may be found at *www.goldenstonepress.com.*

About
the Author

ROBERT SARDELLO, PhD, is cofounder with
Cheryl Sanders-Sardello, PhD, of the School of Spiritual Psychology, which began in 1992. He is author of
Facing the World with Soul, Love and the Soul (reissued as
Love and the World), *Freeing the Soul from Fear, Silence: The
Mystery of Wholeness to the Other,* and *The Power of Soul:
Living the Twelve Virtues.* At the University of Dallas, he
served as chairman of the Department of Psychology,
head of the Institute of Philosophic Studies, and grad-
uate dean. He is also cofounder and faculty member
of the Dallas Institute of Humanities and Culture,
author of more than 200 articles in scholarly journals
and cultural publications, and was on the faculty of the
Chalice of Repose Project in Missoula, Montana.

Having developed spiritual psychology based in
archetypal psychology, phenomenology, and the Spiritual Science of Rudolf Steiner from more than thirty-
five years of research in this discipline, as well as
holding positions in two universities, Sardello is now
an independent teacher and scholar teaching all over
the United States, Canada, and the United Kingdom,
as well as in the Czech Republic, the Philippines, and

Australia. He is a consultant to many educational and cultural institutions, as well as dissertation adviser at numerous academic institutions.